THE THIRTIES REBOOT

ABHINAV BHALLA

INDIA • SINGAPORE • MALAYSIA

ISBN 979-8-89588-384-6

For my late father, who taught me to look up at the stars,

And for my children, Anishka and Kabir, who help me see them anew.

To the generation that guided me,
and to the generation I now guide.

Thank you, Dad, for showing me the light,
even in the darkest of nights.
And thank you, my children, for being the stars,
that illuminate my world, near and far.

This journey is for you.

Contents

Part 3
Initiation

Acknowledgements

Writing this book has been a profound journey of self-discovery and growth, and I am deeply grateful to the many people who have supported, inspired and guided me along the way.

First and foremost, I want to thank my family. To my parents, thank you for the foundation of love and values you have given me and for always believing in me. To my children, Anishka and Kabir, thank you for being my constant source of joy, wonder, and motivation to be the best version of myself. To my partner, Archana, thank you for your unwavering patience, and encouragement throughout the ups and downs of my thirties and the process of writing this book. To my sisters, Sangeeta Bhalla and Deepa Anand, thank you for your unconditional love, support, and the unbreakable bond we share.

I am incredibly fortunate to have a circle of close friends who have been my rocks through the challenges and celebrations of my thirties. Thank you for your unwavering friendship, the laughter, the heart-to-heart conversations, and the countless memories we've shared. Your presence in my life is a true blessing.

I also want to express my heartfelt gratitude to Vanessa Singh, Divya Subramanian, and Soni Singh, who generously provided feedback on early drafts of this book. Your insights, questions, and suggestions have been instrumental in shaping my thoughts and refining my message. Thank you for your time, wisdom, and belief in this project.

To my mentors and colleagues who have guided my professional journey, thank you for your advice, support, and the opportunities you have provided me to learn and grow. Your example and leadership have been pivotal in my development.

I am grateful to the many authors, thinkers, and teachers whose work has informed and inspired my reflections on these pages. Your wisdom and perspectives have enriched my understanding and expanded my horizons.

Finally, I want to thank you, dear reader, for picking up this book and joining me on this journey of exploration and growth. I hope that the insights and experiences shared within these pages will resonate with you, provide solace and guidance, and empower you to embrace your unique path through your thirties and beyond.

Writing this book has been a labour of love and a profound privilege. I am deeply grateful to everyone who has been a part of this journey, directly or indirectly. Your presence, love, and support mean more to me than words can express. Thank you.

In youth from rock to rock I went

From hill to hill, in discontent

Of pleasure high and turbulent,

Most pleas'd when most uneasy;

But now my own delights I make,

My thirst at every rill can slake,

And gladly Nature's love partake

Of thee, sweet Daisy!

From: 'To the Daisy' by William Wordsworth

Introduction

Teenage is the age of exploration. In our twenties, we are in the age of new beginnings. The thirties are the age of course correction and reflection.

If you are in your 30s, rejoice. We are the generation that has witnessed the transition from having no TV to smart TV. We have seen the world move from physical calculators to smartphones. I doubt any age in history will have witnessed such a tremendous shift in their lives. Most of these are a direct result of technological advancement, primarily the internet. The internet now connects us with our family, colleagues, and the world. Yet, we have never been more disconnected from ourselves.

The 30s are a transition from the novelty of the 20s to the stability of the 40s. We must try to let this transition be smooth. However, it needs care and precision. This transition gives you enough chance to introspect and course-correct. Any deviation shown can take you off course and waste a lot of your productive years.

How we live in our thirties defines the rest of our lives. That is the decade when we can garner courage and confidence to start new things. We can also reflect on our choices, which helps us correct our course if need be.

We spend our teenage years exploring, be it our bodies or our career choices. We also explore the themes of love and relationships. During our teens, we are not worried about the far side of life. We are just starting out, and we feel we have the entire lifetime in front of us.

In our twenties, our teenage exploration reaches its destination. Many of us get married and start our journey of matrimony. We also begin our professional lives, take up jobs, change jobs, make new professional associations, form new relationships, find new work friends, and enter new surroundings. Before you know it, the decade is over, and we reach the age of thirty.

Somewhere in our thirties, it hits us that we are nearing our midlife, that our active years are numbered, and that if we have to start something new, it is now or never. We reflect on our choices, we introspect and deep dive into our past and future. We become more conscious about our finances. 'Retirement' and 'retirement planning' are words not absent from our dictionary.

We gain wisdom; we now understand that our actions have consequences, and so do our reactions. Some of us feel blessed for the way things are progressing; some of us curse our choices. These are the choices we made in our teens and twenties, our career and profession, our partner, our spouse, and each and every decision we took that has now shaped the life we are now living.

Our choice of friends, eating choices, lifestyle choices, career choices, and all other choices we make define us, our awareness of ourselves, our projection to the outside world, and the world's perception of us.

This book is my ode to the decade of the thirties. Here, I have expressed the joys, fears, aspirations, and failures that we usually face in our thirties and my reflection on those emotions and events. I have also talked about the ways and methods I adopted to take control of my thoughts and feelings. My reflections have led me to a much fuller life than I would have had I not reflected on my past choices or prepared myself for the future.

I must admit that I have assumed that all of us would go through the same cycle as I have. Still, I believe that most of us follow similar paths and on our trails, the choices we make define our destiny. I do not believe in a predestined life. On the contrary, I fervently believe that every choice we make has consequences. Therefore, our minds should be conditioned to make the correct choice, even unconsciously.

The life cycle that I have mentioned is just a generally accepted norm considering the typical lifespan of a human being. However, with the increase in life expectancy of humans and the changes in the way of thinking and working, these usually accepted timelines have been changing. People are pushing the boundaries, the social pattern is going through a sea change, and because of that, there are no timelines. Things are more in flux, and it is becoming more and more acceptable. For example, from the earlier accepted norm of marrying in your early 20s, it has become acceptable to marry in your late 20s. However, in the recent past, these norms have evolved. It is now quite common to see people marry in their early 30s, late 30s, or not marry at all. Also, with the number of divorces on the rise, having doubled in the last two decades, people have started questioning the future of the institution of marriage as it is traditionally seen.

If you are among those questioning the norms set by society, then you are among the few who dare to stand against societal norms. To make use of this book, being a follower of societal norms is not a prerequisite. You can bring about changes in your life at any point in time.

Remember: *Any time is a good time to bring positive change in your life.*

One may say, who will decide what is correct, what is the benchmark for correct and incorrect choices, or right and wrong choices for that matter? My answer would be, we do it ourselves. We are our benchmark since we are the ones to experience the results of our choices. A choice or decision is not wrong when we make that choice. Only when the outcome of those choices emerges can we say that the choice was wrong. It is in hindsight that we, ourselves, judge our choice to be correct or incorrect, appropriate or inappropriate. What is right for me may be unsuitable for the other person. Still, as long as my conscience has approved my choice, I should be ready to face the consequences that follow.

I can choose to wake up at five in the morning or eight. Once I have made my choice, I should not blame everything wrong in the world for not having had a productive day. I can't blame the traffic, I can't blame the client or customer, I can't blame anybody but myself for missing deadlines. I am just bearing the consequences of my choice.

If I eat unhealthy food, I can't blame my family for bringing junk into the house. What I eat is my choice and my choice alone. If I am swayed by others to make any decision, I have to accept that it was my choice to follow others.

These reflections have helped me take corrective steps, correct my course, and take control of my life. I hope that my reflections will add something positive to everyone who chooses to read this book.

Life is interesting; each day of life is enjoyable. So, do not let your life pass by; take an interest in it; it is waiting for you to do that.

Stay blessed! Stay curious!

Part 1

Inner Reboot

Slow Down

Dheere Dheere re manna, dheere sab kuch hoye,
Maali seenche sau gharha, ritu aaye phal hoye.

- Kabir Das (15th-century mystic poet)

Slowly, O mind! Everything happens at its own pace,

The gardener may put a hundred buckets of water, but fruit will come only in its season.

There is a time in our lives when everything and everyone around us seems to be running. We do not bother to see if they're going anywhere or are just running. If you look closely, it would appear that most are just running without going anywhere. However, when you look around, you tend to feel that you also need to run, lest you fall behind. I was also going through the same routine, running the run, just for the sake of it.

Then the pandemic struck, and before we knew it, the world came to a standstill. Many cities and countries were put under lockdown, and everyone was forced to stop. Things slowed down forcibly, but I had time to reflect on my run, and I was not happy with where I had reached. I realised that I was running on the spot and, in my ignorance, felt satisfied that I was part of the race and maybe would be leaving others behind one day.

It is not about what I had achieved professionally or personally. But it was about what I wanted to achieve. Was I happy to have achieved something and having reached somewhere? Yes. Was it something I wanted and somewhere I wanted to be? No. I realised I was living without reflecting on what, why, and how I was doing it. It was just happening, and I was letting things be.

You get to reflect only when you slow down. When you're running, you only see the track in front of you. Very few people know the goal they are running to; the rest just run. Which one is better? I would say that running can help you achieve more as long as you know where you are going. If you have a definite goal in front of you, then your actions are directed towards that goal. Unfortunately, most people are running without a purpose or plan, like a headless chicken trying to find a way. Such mindless running does not lead you anywhere. Yet, it does drain your energy to give you a feeling of accomplishment without actually achieving anything worthwhile. To triumph over that vain feeling and build awareness of whether you are running in your intended direction or directionless, you need to slow down every now and then.

In other words, you need to be mindful of what you want and what you are doing to achieve those wants. Therefore, being mindful is a means to an end, the end being the goal you wish to achieve. You need to ask the questions, the difficult ones:

What is my goal?
What am I doing to reach my goals?
Why am I doing what I'm doing?
Is it the only way, or is there a more innovative way to do it?
Am I convinced that I am on the right path?

For asking these difficult questions and answering them, you need to slow down every now and then. This is because the answers are within you; you already know the answers to the most challenging questions. But not asking the questions to avoid the answers does not solve the problem; it only prolongs it.

Meditation helps; it increases your awareness. It rests your mind, which enables you to reflect on your day, year, and life. Another thing that helps is the mantra, 'Take Your Time'. After every hour of the day, while drinking water, taking a short walk, any time you are with yourself for 30 seconds to 1 minute, just reflect on what you are doing:

How is it helping me, professionally or personally?
Is there another way to do it, a better way?
Do I need to do it differently?

Waking up early in the morning and setting up a routine for meditation, reflection, and prayer is a wonderful way to set the day's tone. Then, when you work or do anything with more awareness, with more knowledge of why you are doing it, you enjoy the activity more and achieve more productivity. For example, there were many days when I came back from the office and immediately opened my laptop and started working again to get things done.

It went well into the night, and I missed my time with the kids who went off to sleep by then. When I reflected on why I was doing that, I realised one of my biggest mistakes: I did not delegate what I could.

It is not incorrect to say that if you want something done right, do it yourself. But that would leave you with no time to do things that really matter, things you are more competent to do and end up doing more non-productive work. So I started taking small but deliberate steps towards identifying tasks I could delegate. I realised so many things which take little time but add up to take up most of your day.

The results were incredible. I had more time and less stress. You can also use tools like to-do lists or planning apps. They help you keep track, and since you don't have to remember everything, you are more relaxed. So, the key lesson here:

Slow down, every now and then, and reflect. It helps you to be sorted and achieve more of what you want instead of what others want. It will also help you to stop running with others and carve your own path.

Take Your Time

These words may be contrary to what we do most of the time, but they are the most essential words for better productivity. Take your time.

When I ask you to take your time, I do not mean to literally slow the pace of whatever activity you are doing (although it will be interesting to see someone do that). What I really mean is, avoid rushing things. Slow down and reflect:

Why am I in a situation where I need to rush things?

Did I not delegate whatever I could?

Am I trying to multitask?

I believe that multitasking does not help you achieve more; it only enables you to get a shoddy job done, usually in more time.

Pick up things to do one at a time and just get them done before you move on to the next.

The new digital age does not let us do that and wreaks havoc on our concentration and focus. Use features like 'Screen time' and 'Digital well-being' on your handheld devices to control how much and where you are spending your time digitally. YouTube is an addictive platform. It has a feature that can remind you of when it is time to go to sleep; use that feature. Also, turn off the 'Auto Play' feature.

When we take our time to do things slowly, we derive pleasure from the activity. It is not just a task; we enjoy an activity if we can do it well - that's human nature. But we will not be able to do it well unless we spend the time actually required for that work. Skills are not programmes that we can install; we need time to learn a skill and then some more time to implement that skill well.

So, the idea is to avoid rushing things and take time. We have enough time; we just feel we don't. Here are some pointers on how we could remove that feeling that we need to rush things:

- Do not multitask.
- Delegate what you can.
- Slow down and reflect.
- Fix a time for social media.
- Fix a time for checking and responding to emails and messages.

There is another trick that works wonders, **get up early**.

I know many of you would simply want to close this book and go off to your daily routines, but I request you to try it for a few days. This book you are holding is an example of what can happen if you wake up early. That is the time when your creativity is released, your mind is fresh, and you have some time to prime it and make it ready to take on the rest of the day.

One hour in the morning with zero disturbance can help you achieve the equivalent of 3 to 4 hours of work you can usually do during the day. If you think you do not have time, add this one hour to your day and achieve additional productivity of 3 to 4 hours in a day. I do not think there is a better bargain available.

You may already have read or heard about waking up early. I would suggest you give it a go for a few days. You can use this time to:

- Meditate.
- Exercise.
- Plan the rest of your day and prepare your to-do list.

If you are into creative work, do it in the early morning instead of late hours, and the difference in the tone of your work will surprise you. Morning time gives you hope and presents possibilities. It is a joyous time, and that positivity will reflect in your work.

Initially, when you add that important one hour, just sit with yourself and listen to your thoughts. Try to be aware of your thoughts and trust your intuition to lead you to your true path. Then, the rest of the things will follow.

Conclusion

In our fast-paced modern lives, it's easy to get caught up in the frenetic race and lose sight of where we're truly heading. We run and run, often without a clear purpose or destination in mind.

The key lesson here is to deliberately slowdown from time to time. Take moments throughout your day to pause, reflect, and ask yourself the critical questions: What are my goals? What am I doing to reach them? Why am I doing what I'm doing? Is this the best path forward?

Techniques like meditation, making to-do lists, delegating tasks, and focusing on one thing at a time can all help create space for this vital self-reflection. Most importantly, try waking up an hour earlier each day. That distraction-free time is invaluable for planning, creative work, and listening to your inner voice.

When you slow your pace with intention, you can enjoy the journey more while also improving your productivity and results. You gain the clarity to carve your own purposeful path rather than blindly following the herd.

So, take a deep breath. Decelerate. Ask the hard questions and trust your intuition. Slowing down just may be the key to speeding up your progress in the direction you want to go. Small, deliberate changes, consistently applied, will take you further in the long run than racing ahead at an unsustainable pace. Slow down to ultimately go further and faster.

Find a Release

Dil hi to hai na sang-o-khisht, dard kaise na ho,
Gar mi jaan se guzre to kaafir hai agar na roye.

- Mirza Ghalib (1797-1869): Urdu Ghazal (Excerpt)

The heart is not stone or brick, how can it not feel pain? If it (the pain) passes through my soul, it's disbelieving (of humanity) if I don't cry.

Just like an industrial pipe, our mind also gets clogged sometimes with all the dirt that we hear, read, and even think about. Criticism, gossip, and generally the news we hear, the negativity around us, are the dirt that clogs up our mind and stops us from thinking straight.

We may feel different emotions at this time, such as pain, anger, sadness, or a mix of both. Acknowledging and expressing those emotions is important, while denying or suppressing pain and other emotions is unnatural. Letting out these emotions in one way or another helps in several ways:

A. It helps you cope with your intense emotions. Once the emotions have been let out, their intensity decreases. For example, if you have had bouts of anger, you would have noticed that you start feeling calmer once you have let it out on someone. Wouldn't it be better if we let out such negative emotions without hurting others, damaging relationships, and without any feeling of guilt or remorse?

B. Releasing your emotions with the intention of self-discovery helps you churn out the next step you need to take. When we release our emotions constructively, we can look at things objectively without our emotions clouding our judgement. Only then can we look at things as they truly are. Let us take an example to understand this concept. Suppose you have been in the same job for the last six years. You made good progress in the first three years, but you are not getting the growth you expected for the previous three years. That has made you feel unhappy. You want to quit but are afraid that (a) you will lose out on the comfort you have gained in the present job; (b) you will not get the growth/respect/compensation you deserve, and (c) you will need to prove yourself again in the new organisation. If you put down your fears and deal with each one, you might instead realise that (a) it will be a challenge you may enjoy; (b) you are already not getting the growth in the present organisation, and that is your foremost reason for thinking about change, and (c) you are competent because of your work experience till now and proving yourself will not be a problem. This releasing of emotions will give you the confidence to decide, take the next step, or know the next step you need to take.

C. It helps you become more self-aware. For example, when you write down your thoughts and feelings in a journal, you slowly release them. If you are writing for 10 minutes, you take those 10 minutes to go through your emotions. Each minute of writing will make you more aware of your feelings towards those emotions as you release them. Being aware of your feelings gives you the freedom of understanding them and makes a mental note of their utility or triviality. As a result, you are more mindful for those 10 minutes and therefore more in control.

In such times, I have found a few methods that can really work:

Sleep It Off

This is the most uncomplicated and most comfortable of the methods. You may have noticed that we could be really stressed one day, and when we wake up the next day, the stress is gone. In fact, the morning has come with some solution to our problems. Anger and sadness have now turned into positivity and determination.

The phrase 'sleep it off' is not to be taken lightly. It is one of the best things you can do when you feel you are in a situation that you can't really control, but it is stressing you out immensely. There have also been many scientific studies on sleep and how a good night's sleep improves mood. But, unfortunately, the opposite is also true. If you have not had a proper sleep, you will feel irritable and out of sorts.

Exercise

The endorphins released when we exercise can help us stay positive, happy, and satisfied. That is just the mental state we are talking about. The benefits your body will achieve with some regular moderate exercise will be tremendous. I am not saying that you should go and take a one-year membership at a gym. But, just thirty minutes of moderate exercise will give wonderful results for both mind and body. Physical activity is no less than meditation. When you work out or play a sport, you divert your full attention and focus to that physical task; your mind is moving your body. At that time, it is not thinking of any other activity or work. This will build your muscles in both mind and body.

You could also use your exercise time to reflect on your day. For this, you will have to make walking your exercise of choice. Reflect on your previous day or the day gone by if you are going for your walk in the evening, the choices you made, your learnings from the day. This is when you can set an intention for the day ahead or the next day, an intention to be productive, to be happy, and to be a learner.

Many counselling therapies will not achieve what thirty minutes of the solitary walk can do. It is one of the best ways to slow down and reflect and can help you release stress and anxiety.

Write or Draw

I did not realise the benefit of writing down my thoughts until I actually started doing that. It happened by chance when I was attending a course on developing good writing skills. Our instructor, Suma Varughese, asked us to start a daily ten-minute writing exercise to build our writing style. The idea was to look at anything around us and start writing about it and let our mind take us wherever it wishes to. Lo and behold, the exercise to build my writing style became something else, something more. It became my daily release, my daily journal in which I started penning my thoughts. It gave me satisfaction; it gave me direction. It helped me deal with the mental clutter and gave me the clarity I had never experienced.

Connect with Nature

We are part of nature; that is why we feel at peace in our natural surroundings. Which sound will have a calming effect on you, a river flowing or a generator running?

The more you stay in your natural surroundings, the more peaceful you become. I understand that our work and family commitments do not allow us to spend as much time in nature as we would want. Still, we could surely at least take some time to be in nature every day. It could be for your morning walk or exercise, for meditation, or maybe just for sitting in silence for some time. Then, you are likely to feel more relaxed and content for the rest of the day and night.

When you take deliberate steps to release your emotions, you will automatically be more aware and, therefore, more in control of your emotions the next time you are going through an emotional state. More control of your emotions would mean you have gained new options in your life that you never thought existed. You can now:

- Embrace your positive emotions.
- Reframe your thoughts to better suit your needs and surroundings.
- Manoeuvre negative emotions towards a more positive outlook.
- In the process, gain more happiness.

Happiness, of course, is the real wealth we seek through different ways and means. Depending on how our environment has programmed our minds, we may be looking for happiness in money, power, family, or fame and recognition. However, these are just means for the ultimate goal we all seek: to be happy.

If you slow down for a moment and ask yourself what you really want, you will know about your desires. If you delve deeper and lead your questioning from 'what?' to 'why?', you will be directed to your actual need:

What do I want?
I want more money.

Why do I want more money?
To be able to buy and have all the things that I desire.

Why do I want to buy all the things that I desire?
To feel happy.

Take any desire or want of yours and ask the question 'why?' and it will ultimately lead you to your need to be happy. Happiness is our ultimate desire.

Conclusion

Our minds, much like industrial pipes, can get clogged with the dirt and negativity that we absorb from the world around us. Criticism, gossip, and distressing news can build up inside us, leading to intense emotions such as anger, sadness, and pain.

While it may feel unnatural, acknowledging and releasing these emotions is crucial for our well-being. Suppressing them will only cause the pressure to build. Finding a healthy release valve allows us to lower the intensity, gain objectivity and develop greater self-awareness.

Strategies like sleeping on a problem, exercising, journaling, talking with a friend, or getting creative can all serve as effective ways to process difficult feelings. The key is to let the emotions flow out constructively, without judgement.

As we release our pent-up feelings, we create space for fresh perspectives and solutions to emerge. We start to see our challenges more clearly, unburdened by the weight of our initial reactions. Releasing emotions with the intention of self-discovery can unveil important insights about our needs, fears, and path forward.

Most importantly, finding a regular release for our emotions builds our resilience and empowers us to navigate life's ups and downs with greater equanimity. We learn to ride the waves without getting pulled under by their intensity.

Releasing our emotions is not about instantly fixing our problems. It's about loosening their grip on us so that we can chart our course ahead with a clearer mind and a more peaceful heart. By developing the habit of acknowledging and releasing our feelings, we safeguard our well-being and allow our best selves to shine through.

The next time you feel the tell-tale pressure building inside, remember that releasing it is not only okay – it's necessary. Find the release that works for you and let it flow. On the other side awaits a lighter, brighter version of you.

Happiness

Sukh duhkh do pahariya, rain din baraat jaat.
Man changa to kathin kaam bhee sukhadaayak hot.

- Kabir Das (15th-century mystic poet)

Suffering and happiness are like two wheels. Night and day pass by like this.

If the mind is pure, even difficult tasks become enjoyable.

Happiness is the most sought-after feeling in our lives. Ultimately, every human being wants to be happy. But there is a problem; we do not know (a) how to be happy and then (b) how to stay happy. Since we are not sure how to achieve happiness, we try to find it in different ways.

Most of us think that happiness can be found in things. People who do not have money feel that if they get money, they will be happy. People who are wealthy, or have money, think that they want some peace in their lives, and then they will be satisfied. So we keep chasing happiness without realising that we will never be able to catch it as long as we chase after it.

Happiness is like a moving goalpost, and most of us fail to hit the target. We just keep on running from one end to the other, from one task to the other, from one goal to the other, hoping that we will find something that will give us happiness one day. If you are that person, I have news for you: happiness can never be achieved; it is not for anyone to conquer, but it can undoubtedly be found. For that, you do not have to look out but inside.

All this time, you are looking for happiness in the wrong places. Joy, however, is within you, and you only need to tap into it. You are an endless source of energy and happiness. Once you realise that, you will no longer need to chase after it. While we are at it, I will tell you a secret. Once you have tapped into the endless happiness within you and start feeling the joy of this life, you will start noticing a change in your everyday life. The world will start looking more habitable, the people will seem to have your best interest at heart, and everything will appear to fall into place. This, when you experience it, will feel like magic, but the truth is that you would be experiencing the law of attraction. Being joyful attracts more joy, more positivity, more love and more of all other positive aspects.

Considering all these brilliant results expected, why wouldn't people be more joyful? But, of course, it is easier said than done. Most of us are slaves to our feelings and emotions. We do not decide how we would feel in a particular situation or on a specific day.

We do not determine our circumstances. For example, suppose we are stuck in a bad relationship or any other condition that does not allow us to be happy. Then, how can we be and feel anything except all the negative emotions such as sadness, disgust, envy, jealousy, and even helplessness?

I agree that we cannot control all our external factors, circumstances, and situations. For most of us, our belief in happiness or lack of it is decided by external factors. Once we have made up our minds, we succumb to the negative emotions that are easier to understand in such a situation. Those negative emotions will have a field day as they take over our mind and body. What do we do then? How do we find happiness within? Since, as I have mentioned time and again, it all starts in our mind, we need to find a way to our emotions and feelings through more awareness and control of our mind.

Mindfulness

Mindfulness is more than just meditation. It is a state of mind which is more in tune with our feelings and emotions. Of course, the path to achieving mindfulness is through meditation. Once you have gained some degree of awareness through regular meditation practice, you will be able to observe your feelings. This allows you to think about why you are feeling the way you are and then detach your emotions from the external circumstances that cause that feeling.

The mind is the most powerful tool given to us by nature. But, as with every tool, we can either use it constructively, let it stay unused, or, even worse, use it destructively.

When we are being mindful and using our brain and body to create something, we are constructive. However, when we are passive, such as when watching TV, we are not really resting our mind but only keeping it unused; we are letting it rust out rather than wear out.

The mind is destructive when we let our negative feelings and emotions take over and control it. Having said that, I do not mean that if you are not mindful, you will not experience happiness. You will experience the whole array of emotions, from happiness and excitement to sadness and anxiety. However, the advent and departure of all these emotions will be automatic and uncontrolled. You will experience these emotions, and your life, like a helpless spectator.

A growth mindset is essential for both personal and professional development. You will need to be open to learning, be flexible in your approach, and keep yourself motivated even when the circumstances are adverse. With mindfulness, you will be more aware and, therefore, in a position to remould your thoughts, your habits, and over a period of time, your mindset. Therefore, in a way, the key to happiness and also success is mindfulness.

Acceptance

Circumstances keep changing. If you let circumstances define you, your nature and your feelings, you will end up like a pendulum, moving from one end of the spectrum to the other. One day you will be served a good breakfast, and you will be happy. Another day, you will be making a burnt toast for yourself, feeling unhappy and frustrated. What can you do to avoid being a pendulum of emotions? Accept the circumstances. By acceptance, I do not mean surrendering to them. If you submit to a situation, you are unlikely to take any action to change that situation. If instead, you accept the situation for what it is, you will gain the ability to look at it distantly. With a bird's-eye view of the situation, you will gain a broader perspective and an option of working on the situation rather than its consequences.

It is essential to understand our emotions since we spend most of our energy on them. That's what emotions are: energy in motion. If you let negative emotions take the best of you, you will feel tired, as if your energy has been sapped. You will feel groggy and frustrated. On the other hand, when you are feeling positive, you will be doubly vibrant and enthusiastic.

Don't let circumstances sap your energy. Instead, accept the situation and maintain a balanced state of mind. This will help you get out of most sticky situations.

In fact, acceptance is the first step for bringing about any kind of change in your life. You can only change what you accept as something that needs changing. Change requires you to accept your flaws and take steps to overcome some of those.

You will learn from situations only when you are receptive, and you will be more receptive only when you are more aware of the circumstances. You will be more aware only when you have accepted the situation and are mindful of its possible consequences.

Learn to be a learner, and you will never have bad experiences in your life, only good learnings.

Remember: *Bad experiences make for good learning*

Challenges

Believe it or not, new challenges can really give our energy a boost and make us happy. It is not about conquering the challenge but the process of going through it that provides us with the required dose of dopamine, leading to increased endorphins. In other words, challenges make us happy. Imagine having all that you desire and nothing left for you to achieve. Would that make you happy? No. Such a situation will make you restless and unhappy. So you will look for new beginnings, new challenges, anything to make you learn or do new things, deal with new situations, make new connections.

New desires and challenges faced in pursuing those desires are essential for our mental health and happiness. A person with no challenges will waste their time on frivolous activities, which might keep them busy for a few days, maybe a few weeks or a few months. Eventually, that person will feel a void, an urge to start something new, something that will throw some challenges their way. To stay happy, never settle; keep challenging yourself.

Look Within

External happiness is ephemeral and of a fleeting nature. It comes and goes and never sticks. One moment you will be happy, and then your bag of worries will overpower you in the next. For lasting happiness, you don't have to look far but look within. First of all, you will have to be happy with yourself. Stop finding faults in yourself. You are a miraculous creature. Your life is a miracle.

Have faith in yourself. Have faith that the universe and nature will support you. Trust yourself and make happiness a habit. Stop waiting for circumstances to change. Stop expecting that having things will make you happy. Circumstances are like waves; good times are followed by unpleasant ones, and the cycle goes on. New things and objects will get old very quickly. New experiences are new only when experienced for the first time. Learn to be happy with yourself, look within, and find joy within yourself, and external happiness will follow. Dire circumstances will stop intimidating you, and eventually, circumstances will change for the better without you even noticing. Once you have turned your mind towards positivity, you will start interpreting circumstances in a manner that favours you. Your interpretation of circumstances becomes your truth. Most life events are either good, bad, or neutral depending on our outlook towards life during that time.

Suppose you're trying to get a contract that would make you a lot of money, and you lost that contract to someone else. One way of looking at it is that you have actually lost something and could feel devastated having to bear that loss. Another way is to understand it as a notional loss since that contract was never yours. You cannot lose what you don't have. The latter outlook will allow you to get over the incident quickly and move on to the next adventure.

Happiness, therefore, is a state of mind. Once you learn the art of minding your mind, happiness is within your reach, and you are on your way to a more fulfilling life.

Conclusion

Happiness is not a destination but a way of travelling. It's not something we can postpone until we reach certain milestones or acquire specific possessions. True happiness emerges from within, from the choices we make and the perspectives we cultivate every day.

While we can't control every circumstance in our lives, we always have a choice in how we respond. We can choose to focus on gratitude, kindness, and the present moment. We can opt to forgive, to let go of comparisons, and to embrace imperfection. These small mindset shifts can profoundly impact our overall happiness and resilience.

It's also important to remember that happiness is not a constant state. Like all emotions, it comes and goes in waves. The goal is not to cling to happiness, but to develop a deeper sense of contentment and equanimity that allows us to weather life's inevitable ups and downs.

Ultimately, happiness is a skill we can cultivate through consistent practice. By setting intentions, celebrating small wins, and surrounding ourselves with positive influences, we create the conditions for happiness to flourish. It's about progress, not perfection.

At the same time, it's crucial not to make happiness another item on our to-do list. The irony is that the more we chase happiness, the more elusive it becomes. Instead, we must learn to let happiness find us in the midst of our ordinary moments and daily routines.

Perhaps the greatest secret to happiness is to stop waiting for it to arrive and start embodying it here and now. Smile more. Worry less. Appreciate the simple joys. Help others. Do more of what lights you up. These are the keys that unlock the door to a happier life.

In the end, happiness is an inside job. It's up to each of us to take responsibility for our well-being and consciously choose the attitudes and actions that support it. By making happiness a habit and a way of being, we not only enrich our own lives, but also inspire others to do the same. And that may be the greatest happiness of all.

Fear

- Kabir Das (15th-century mystic poet)

The penalty of having received this body is experienced by one and all.

The learned bears knowledge, the ignorant cries

Says Kabir, "I would fear if it happened only to me."

Death, old age, and problems happen to everyone.

Oh man, why do you act, and why do you regret your actions?

If you sow a plant of acacia, how will you eat mangoes?

During my journey through my thirties, I realised that the single most significant factor that held me back from doing things the way I intended to do was fear. Fear, ranging from being misunderstood when I post something on my social media handles to the fear of failing to start something new, something challenging. When at your door, fear will eat you from inside and will not let you move forward.

If you feel that you have let fears dictate your life for far too long, it is time for you to give positivity a chance. If you let your worries reign, they will keep getting powerful by eating into you.

The best way, for me, was to take small steps towards allaying those fears, and my method consisted of some known and some unknown components:

- Affirmations
- Small Steps
- Identify the Cause of Your Fears
- Support

Affirmations

Our mind is already full, full of our fears and anxieties. Affirmation is one method in which we can make space for positive beliefs in ourselves, which will remove the negatives and fill our mind space with positives.

We are the results of our thoughts. There have been so many instances when my fear of failure stopped me from starting something new. Affirmations will help you develop positive beliefs by hammering those thoughts and beliefs into your subconscious. They are highly effective in changing our thought processes. Once our thought process changes, our mindset changes, and our way of working shifts towards better.

The conscious and the subconscious mind work in tandem. Both are complementary and supplementary to each other. Our conscious thoughts, feelings, and emotions signal our state of mind to our subconscious. Our subconscious considers our conscious thoughts to be our commands, reinforces them, and creates our world for us, which reflects our thoughts. If you get stuck in the circle of negative thoughts, feelings, and emotions, your subconscious will take it as your command and reinforce those thoughts by creating more negativity around you. The only way to get out of that loop is to change your thoughts and your thought patterns. That is where affirmations come in.

Affirmations are nothing but training for your subconscious. They work the same way as fear. When we fear something, we keep thinking about that fear; we believe in negatives – 'I may fail in this', 'I am not sure if I am built for this task', 'I do not have enough money', 'I am not able to earn money', 'I am not capable of doing this task', 'I might get trolled for this', 'I may be made fun of if I do that', etc.

These thoughts are nothing but a result of how our mind has been conditioned from the time we are born. Even unknowingly, we are shown that the possibility of failure is imminent. Don't do this, don't do that, you may fail, you will fail, you will not be able to do it, you are not made for this, etc.

Our subconscious starts believing that those fears are real, and that holds us back.

When you affirm positive thoughts, the results start showing in a short time. The method is easy: make a list of positive beliefs around which you would want to live your life. These could be related to a particular task that you have been unable to undertake due to some fears, for example,

I am a good writer.
I can express myself.
Words come easily to me.

These affirmations could help you avoid any fears you have as a writer. Affirmations can also be non-specific, and you may use words like,

I am confident.
I can get things done.
I am capable.
I can take on and execute complex tasks.

"Whether you think you can, or you think you can't - you are right"

– Henry Ford

Henry Ford's words are the absolute truth and apply to each of us in our lives now more than ever. Science, through various research, has also put its stamp of acceptance on the effectiveness of affirmations. I would not suggest getting into the scientific significance of this method. Instead, try doing this for a month and see the difference it makes to your thinking pattern.

Spend ten minutes each in the morning as soon as you wake up and right before you sleep, repeating your affirmations in your mind. These are the times when your mind is most receptive, and your subconscious is listening. Give it thoughts that you would want it to retain during these times.

One highly effective method for enjoying the benefits of affirmations is by listening to them. You can record your affirmations on your phone, turn on the repeat mode on the voice note, put on some comfortable earphones, and play the recorded affirmations.

You should be able to see changes in your thinking within two to three weeks. Regular practice of affirming positive thoughts will help you make this way of thinking a permanent part of you. After that, no matter the adversity you may face, your mind will think in the way you have been training it to think.

As a bonus, positive thinking acts as a magnet for more positivity. Expect to find more friends who will support and guide you in your journey.

Small Steps

If you fear taking the leap of faith, take small steps to move towards your goal. When you feel confident and comfortable and feel that your goal is within reach, when you have moved some distance forward and rested some of your fears, that will be the time to take that leap. For example, if you are in a job and wish to start your own business, start using your evenings and weekends to start working on your project. These steps could include reading about how to start a business, reading up on the particular field that you wish to work in, or joining a beginner course on entrepreneurship, joining online communities, finding and talking to similarly placed people, talking to someone around you who may have already done what you plan to do.

However, theory, unless implemented practically, is of no actual use. You will then need to take small practical steps. For example, if you plan to open a restaurant, maybe plan a food truck over weekends. If you plan to open an online store, maybe work on sourcing your products, deciding upon pricing, logistics, etc.

Along with small practical steps to reach your intended goal, you will also need to bring about small behavioural changes, small changes in your daily routine that are in line with your beliefs and your goals. A sea change is a combination of tiny drops of changes that you bring about in your life. For example, small changes in your time management, learning, and actions bring you closer to your goals. This, combined with changes in your belief system, is the only way to bring about changes and achieve your goals.

As long as you do not fear a particular task, you will be able to try that task, and you cannot achieve anything unless you try.

Identify the Cause of your Fears

Can you solve any problem unless you know the cause of that problem? For example, if there is a leakage problem in your house, you will need to find the source of that leakage. Unless you know the source of the leakage, anything you do will only be a temporary fix. This stop-gap arrangement is unlikely to sustain for long.

You will need to introspect: what is holding me back? What is it I am afraid of? Going to the root of your fear is crucial since it gives you the proper perspective and helps you heal. Question yourself: am I afraid of failing or what others would think if I failed? Am I afraid of taking the leap, or am I afraid of letting my family down? Ask yourself these hard questions and seek the answers from within you. Identify your real fears. Unless you do that, you will not be able to address the root cause of your fears.

For me, my biggest fear was not being good enough in my parents' eyes, especially my father. That fear played such a significant role in my mind that I refused to take forward steps, thinking that I would not be good enough if I failed. The result was that I was holding myself back, which eventually meant that I proved to myself that I was not good enough.

Another thing that such fear does to you is that you become a follower; you choose the easy option, a way out. You would want to avoid making decisions and let others do that for you. Then, if you fail, you have the option to blame others. It takes conscious effort to overcome such well-laid fears. Taking small, deliberate steps makes your subconscious start believing in your abilities. It will stop resisting after some time, and you will be in a situation where you will not have to be a person defined by your fears but by your positive actions.

Support

We are social animals. We want to be around people; we want to be admired, loved, and respected. There is no harm in having those needs as long as those needs are not the force driving our actions. If we are acting only to fulfil our need to be loved and respected, we are feeding our fears and asking the wrong questions – what if I am not loved/admired/respected? Our actions and decisions will reflect our need for admiration. The decision may or may not turn out to be correct, but the premise will undoubtedly be incorrect and more harmful in the long run.

There are all sorts of people in the world and, invariably, you will have a variety of people around you. Avoid people who gossip. Gossiping can feed your fears since you may end up thinking that the way you were talking about someone behind their back, you would be spoken about behind your back. Such an expectation can lead you to take unsuitable action. Such small-mindedness can prevent you from following your true purpose, acting with a purity of thought and getting things done.

Finding the right people to be around you can help you make better decisions. Support from positive people who will feed into your positive side and not your fears. Find and be with people who speak positively about others, especially when those people are not in the room. Your mind is a pond, and your thoughts are the fishes that swim in that pond. Do not let some dirty fishes spoil the entire pond. Instead, feed your mind the right food, the food of pure positive thoughts, whether those thoughts are a result of your external or internal factors.

Find support in positive people who may not guide you but are willing to stand by you for the right reasons, who do not write you off for making a hard but appropriate decision.

Be ready and willing to take advice from experienced people, but make sure that the person providing the guidance is the right person. For example, if you are planning to start a business and your guide does not have any experience running a business, then be wary of the advice you are getting. A piece of well-meaning advice can lead you down the wrong path if not taken from the right person.

Your support system is your friends and family. It could be your spouse, your sibling, or parents, or your close friends who will push you on and not strike you down. If you can discuss your fears and apprehensions with someone who can just listen and not dismiss your concerns as baseless, you have found support in that person. If you cannot find such support or are initially afraid of opening up to someone, try to find a release in some other manner. I suggest the journal writing exercise. When you pen down your fears, your mind will lead you to the cause of those fears and ultimately to the steps you need to take to overcome those fears.

Remember: *Answers to all our questions are within us. We just need to learn to listen to our inner voice.*

Whatever you do, understand that it takes concerted effort to overcome your fears, and you are not alone in your journey. Your peers, friends, colleagues, contemporaries, everyone has to deal with their own fears. So affirm positive thinking, take small steps, identify the cause of your fears, find support, and keep moving forward.

Conclusion

Fear is a natural and inevitable part of the human experience. It's an emotion that has evolved to keep us safe from threats, both real and perceived. However, when fear takes hold, it can paralyse us and keep us from living our fullest lives.

The key to overcoming fear is not to eliminate it entirely but to develop a new relationship with it. By acknowledging and befriending our fears, we can learn to use them as a compass rather than a roadblock. Our fears can point us towards the very things we need to do to grow and thrive.

One of the most powerful tools for navigating fear is to reframe it as excitement. Physiologically, fear and excitement are almost identical. The only difference is our mental label. By consciously choosing to view our fear as excitement, we can channel that energy into positive action.

Another essential strategy is to break our fears down into manageable steps. Rather than getting overwhelmed by the enormity of our fears, we can focus on taking one small, courageous step at a time. Each micro-bravery builds our confidence and momentum, making the next step easier.

It's also crucial to remember that courage is not the absence of fear, but the willingness to act in spite of it. Some of the most successful and fulfilled people are those who have learnt to feel the fear and do it anyway. They understand that on the other side of fear lies growth, possibility, and aliveness.

Ultimately, overcoming fear is an ongoing practice. It requires self-compassion, patience, and a commitment to facing our fears repeatedly. It means choosing courage over comfort and embracing the discomfort of the unfamiliar.

The irony is that when we run from our fears, they tend to grow larger and more powerful. But when we turn to face them, we often discover that they are not as scary as we imagined. In fact, our greatest fears can become our greatest teachers, revealing the depths of our strength and resilience.

The next time fear arises, remember that it's a normal part of the journey. Take a deep breath, acknowledge the fear, and then take one small step forward. Trust that you have the capacity to handle whatever lies ahead, and know that with each courageous step, you are expanding your comfort zone and creating a life of greater freedom and fulfilment.

Fear is not the enemy. It's a signpost pointing us towards the very things we need to do to become our best selves. By learning to embrace and navigate fear, we open ourselves up to a world of boundless possibility. And that is truly a life worth living.

Positive Thinking

Manopubbaṅgamā dhammā
Manoseṭṭā manomayā
Manasā ce pasannena
Bhāsati vā karoti vā
Tato naṃ sukhamanveti
Chāyaā'va anapāyinī.

– Dhammapada 1:2

Our life is shaped by our mind; we become what we think. Joy follows a pure thought like a shadow that never leaves.

(Translation from The 'Dhammapada' by Eknath Easwaran)

As we grow, our mind evolves. Many of us grow wiser; many of us stay rooted in the past. The past is a reflection of what we were, not what we will be and definitely not what we ought to be. But our past does hold us back. Our past experiences can hold us down. We need to reimagine our present and future to reach our true potential and not be stuck in the past.

What you sow is what you will reap. So let your imagination of your present and your future be positive and fulfilling. Let it be full of gratitude for your life and what you have achieved so far. Let it be full of thoughts of well-being for yourself and for others. If your mind is filled with negative thoughts, you will see that negativity in everything around you. You will end up experiencing that negativity in your life. You will have nothing to be grateful for. The gift of life you have received will be worthless since you have nothing good to experience in this life.

Initially, it will take a deliberate effort to think positively and be grateful for being alive. Then, you will need to learn to shift your energies towards thinking about all the good things you have, things you have achieved over the last ten, twenty years, and all the good things you are bound to achieve. You can read as many books as possible and stories on positive thinking and the power it holds. You can read up on how positive thinking leads to a positive outcome and how your desires manifest before you based on your thoughts. It is not a new concept. It has been out there for centuries. With the speed and ease of information dissipation today, more people are now coming across the idea and realising its true power, its true meaning. However, it will not work unless you actually implement it.

What if you are faced with an adverse situation? There will undoubtedly be situations in your life when you can't keep yourself calm, when you can't think of anything positive. You will forget, in those moments, the healing powers of positive thinking. Those will be the moments that will define you and your strength. It will depend on how quickly you can come out of the negative state of mind.

Sometimes, a negative state of mind could also give a false sense of bliss to the person suffering; an ecstatic feeling in resigning to the situation, cursing and blaming everything and everyone, and acting out instead of getting the act together.

There are a few things that can be done to save yourself from getting into an adverse situation and, if you find yourself in one, to ensure you do not stay stuck in a negative state of mind longer than you have to:

- Keep your life simple.
- Stay constructive.
- Reframe your thoughts.
- Affirm and visualise.

Keep Your Life Simple

If you overcomplicate your life, expect more negative situations. Examples of over-complicated lives could include family disputes, power tussles, extra-marital relationships, etc. It is better to strike such complicated issues at the root. If you are in a complicated relationship, whether personal or professional, get out of it or reach a settlement that works for all parties involved. I know it is not easy, and it requires at least one person in such a conflict to let go of their ego. It is also possible that you may feel let down by yourself. Others may take you to be a cowardly being. That is where your mental strength will need to be invoked. The power that positive thinking holds will need to be summoned.

The simplicity of life will reward you. Whatever actual or notional loss you may experience will be compensated with mental peace, which will help you achieve much more. I have seen people being stuck in such hostile situations for years with no end in sight. Your life will thank you if you just start taking steps in the positive direction to get out of such a situation.

Similarly, suppose you are stuck in the wrong business relationship. In that case, it is better to bear some loss and get over it than to lose your mind and be stuck in that situation, which can damage you further.

I am not saying that you do not take steps to salvage a situation going downhill. All I am saying is that when all your efforts in a positive direction have failed, it is time to cut your losses and move out before it is too late. Do not let your ego dictate how long you will bear a negative situation.

The relief of leaving behind your past will be rewarding in more ways than one.

The simplicity of life also means that you do not try to manipulate others. If you have a simple and positive mindset, you will find the right people with the right attitude. In addition, a simple life will prevent you from getting into a bad situation.

If, despite positive thinking and simple living, you end up in a difficult situation that you cannot or could not have avoided, then what can you do? After all, not everything that happens in your life is controlled by you: Find something constructive to do.

Stay Constructive

When you find yourself in an adverse situation beyond your control, you can come out of it by doing something creative and constructive. The human race is inherently creative. Our mind is built to create, and when it doesn't, it feels out of place, as if something is not correct. In our personal and professional lives, we feel the need to create something better or more than what exists.

You will need to give your mind its solace by finding something constructive to do. Creating something is the biggest gift you can give yourself. That creation is the result of being productive. Join a charity, pick up a new hobby, or start a new website. Anything you create will let you move into a positive mindset and bring you back into a positive lifestyle.

It is a cycle; if you are in a negative situation, you start thinking negatively. Then, everything around you begins to appear negative. Soon, you observe more negative things happening to you. Then you remember all the negative things that have happened to you in the past. Finally, you feel disheartened and disillusioned, and you think that nothing good can happen in your life, and then life grants you that wish.

Finding that rope that lets you climb out of negativity is essential. Meditate, imagine a positive outcome, and you are bound to find that rope and not get stuck in a negative circle. In effect, be careful what you wish for.

Reframe Your Thoughts

*"When you change the way you look at things,
the things you look at change."*

– Max Planck

If I were to ask you to think of any one person in your life who matters to you. It could be a colleague, a friend, your spouse, a relative or your domestic help, for that matter. Then I want you to list, in your mind, the good and bad qualities of that person. Can there be any person with only good or bad characteristics? I can say with conviction that you will be able to think of both good and bad features of that person. What you focus on really makes all the difference. If you focus on the good, you will see the good and think of good things about that person. Similarly, focusing on bad qualities will lead you to think of unpleasant things about the same person. Suppose a person is honest and lazy. For you, depending on your focus, that person could be an honest person or a lazy person. If you direct your focus on honesty, you will have a positive image of that person in your mind. The opposite will apply if you focus on laziness.

The person has not changed; they remain the same, but your viewpoint changes, and based on that, your thoughts change and therefore, your view of that person changes. It is possible that at any point in time, depending on how you are feeling at a particular time, you may see the good or the bad aspects of that person. That is what needs to change. Focusing on the positives will encourage and energise you, while focusing on the negatives will discourage and dishearten you. When the person is the same, and that person hasn't changed, and we are already aware of their qualities, how can that same person appear different to us at different times?

What do you think will happen if you come across some quality of that person that disgusts you, frustrates you, or irritates you? What if, at that very moment, you direct your thoughts to the good in that person? Suddenly, your focus will shift, and so will your feelings, leading to instant relief and relaxation from what was troubling you.

There are certain character traits which can be interpreted negatively and positively. For such character traits, you may have to change your interpretation of that characteristic itself. For example, if the other person comes across as too ambitious, it can be seen as a good or bad quality, and it is up to you how you look at it. For example, if you are looking for a business partner, an ambitious person could be seen either positively or negatively depending on your own thinking, needs, circumstances, and earlier experiences. In such a situation, it is possible that even though your earlier personal experience may differ, your business requirements may need such a person to complement your own qualities. This is when you will be interpreting ambition in a different light. However, you will not have that option for most facets. You will have to change your focus rather than changing interpretation.

This process of reframing your thoughts also applies to all the situations you face every day. Reframe your thoughts, and you will start feeling that your surroundings have changed.

Affirm and Visualise

When you were younger, you must have heard people advising you, especially your parents, to surround yourself with good, positive people. "Be in the company of good people," "A person is known by the company they keep," "Choose your friends wisely." The idea may have been that being with the wrong people will lead you down the wrong path, and they were right. Have you ever felt different energy around optimistic and positive people and an opposite kind of energy around negative people or even places? That is because positive people release positive energy, which can be felt; it is palpable. The same goes for negative thoughts and people. How can you stay positive then? Just by being with positive people? No, that is not enough. Your thoughts need to be positive. So how do you do that? Use the power of affirmations and visualisation.

Affirmations are concise and precise positive beliefs that you repeat to yourself. Visualisation is a technique through which you visualise your present or future. When you combine affirmation and visualisation, they are powerful enough to let you release positive energies, which eventually lead you to become what you visualised and affirmed.

Focus on one goal that you want to achieve and direct your affirmations and visualisations towards that goal. Your actions will follow your thoughts in everyday life as long as you are saying and listening to your affirmations every day, at least once. If you want to become an excellent public speaker, your affirmation could be:

I am confident
I am a good storyteller.

Do not bring negative connotations into your affirmations. For example, instead of saying, "I do not fear the unknown," say, "I am courageous. I embrace the unknown."

When you combine visualisation with your affirmations, they become more powerful. Visualisation is the act of imagining yourself as having achieved the beliefs and actions you set out to achieve.

As you visualise, you need to feel the way you would once you have achieved your goal. Feel the exhilaration and excitement of achievement. Feel good about life, yourself, and everything you have in your life.

What happens after that? Do you get what you visualise? No, not just yet. Affirmations and visualisation have to be followed up with positive, committed action. If positive thoughts are not followed up with positive action, then you are only just daydreaming. Your thoughts will implore you to take action. It will not matter if you do not know the way or the path to choose. That will come later. Now is the time to take action.

Take small steps if you do not know where you are going, and you are sure to find the path you will need to follow. The universe will show you the way; you will start seeing the signs. You will start finding the right people, guides who will help you in your journey. Things do not fall into place on their own. You will need to follow this three-step process conscientiously to see positive change in your life.

Affirm

Visualise

Act

If you want to get fit, visualising yourself as fit will not help unless you improve your diet and exercise. Likewise, if you wish to be wealthy, visualising it will not help unless you take control of your finances and make progress in your work by advancing your skills and persevering.

The process of positive thinking helps you in achieving your goals. For example, if you think, 'no matter what I do, I can't get fit or wealthy', then whether you like it or not, you will visualise yourself as unfit and poor. Your actions will follow your thought process since your mind has already decided on the end result.

If you reverse the process, if you start thinking positively, your actions will follow your thoughts, and positive change will follow.

The process is not easy, but it is not difficult either. It requires persistence and good control of your mind. That control comes from training your mind, which comes from meditation. So, if you have been having trouble keeping up with your plans of developing self-control or self-discipline, my suggestion is that you start with meditation. Once you reach the stage of feeling more in control of your mind, the rest of your life will follow you instead of you following life and letting it take you wherever it wants. You will be more in control of everyday aspects of your life, and before you know it, you will be living a fuller, more satisfying life.

Conclusion

Positive thinking is not about denying reality or ignoring life's challenges. Rather, it's about consciously choosing to focus on the good, even in the face of adversity. It's about training our minds to look for the opportunity in every difficulty and to believe in our own resilience and resourcefulness.

The power of positive thinking lies in its ability to shape our experiences and outcomes. When we approach life with a positive mindset, we tend to see more possibilities, attract more positive people and circumstances, and bounce back more quickly from setbacks. Our thoughts create our reality.

One of the most effective ways to cultivate positive thinking is through the practice of gratitude. By regularly acknowledging and appreciating the good in our lives, we shift our attention away from lack and toward abundance. We train our brains to scan for the positive, which can quickly become a self-fulfilling prophecy.

Another key strategy is to watch our self-talk. The way we speak to ourselves matters deeply. By catching negative self-talk and consciously replacing it with more supportive and encouraging messages, we can fundamentally reshape our inner landscape. Over time, this practice of positive self-talk can become second nature.

It's also important to surround ourselves with positive influences, whether that's uplifting books, inspiring role models, or supportive friends and family members. The more we immerse ourselves in positivity, the more it becomes our default way of being.

At the same time, positive thinking is not about suppressing or denying negative emotions. It's about acknowledging them, learning from them, and then consciously shifting our focus towards solutions and growth. It's about developing the resilience to face challenges with optimism and hope.

Ultimately, positive thinking is a choice we make in every moment. It's a muscle we can strengthen through consistent practice. By choosing to focus on the good, believe in ourselves, and look for the lesson in every setback, we become the architects of our own reality.

The power of positive thinking extends far beyond our own lives. When we embody positivity, we naturally inspire and uplift others. We become a force for good in the world, spreading hope and possibility wherever we go.

The next time you find yourself slipping into negative thinking, remember that you have the power to choose a different path. Take a deep breath, find something to appreciate, and shift your focus towards the good. Trust that by aligning your thoughts with your highest intentions, you will attract experiences and outcomes that match that vibration.

Positive thinking is not a panacea for all of life's problems. But it is a powerful tool for navigating those problems with greater ease, resilience, and joy. By making positive thinking a way of life, you open yourself up to a world of limitless potential. And that is a truly empowering way to live.

Self-Awareness

Khudi ko kar buland itna ki har taqdeer se pehle,
Khuda bande se poochhe bata teri raza kya hai?

– Allama Muhammad Iqbal (20th century poet, philosopher, and political activist)

Elevate your self-awareness so much that even before destiny arrives,

God asks the man, "Tell me, what is your wish?"

An essential aspect of my being has been how others look at me, what is my image in the eyes of others. My actions were often defined by how I was perceived by others for those actions. It took me a while to understand the foolishness of that thought process. Finally, I realised that, in fact, my efforts were defined by my perception of how others would perceive my actions.

I was pre-empting the thoughts of others and applying those notions to myself. Thus, my decisions and actions were a direct consequence of my skewed imagination of how others would see such a decision or action.

More often than not, I was living my life through the eyes of others. My motivation was my image, and when we talk about an image, it is only a reflection and has nothing to do with our true self.

How I dressed was motivated by how others would see me. How and what I spoke of was encouraged by how others would see me. My introspection then led me to two conclusions:

No other person has time to spend on me or my image.

It is a fleeting world where things are moving, at least they seem to be moving, at the speed of light, a direct result of the digital age with its content and social media.

In this apparently fast-paced life, no one has a minute to spare for anybody else. The age-old wisdom still holds true that you are alone in this life, and you will have to walk alone. The thoughts that others are watching me or listening to me are just out of my desire to be considered significant. How can that be anything but the imagination of my own importance? It is a result of my desire to feel and be considered important. It is my ego taking control of my thinking.

This circle of desire to be considered of value, leading to the imagination of importance and living our life based on such a vision, will never be broken unless you overcome its root cause, i.e., the desire to be seen and heard by others. You will need to start listening to yourself and looking at yourself as you are without the screen of ego clouding your vision. You will need to understand and accept your deepest emotions, and that is called self-awareness.

Your awareness of your own being, your natural self, sets you free. You let go of inhibitions. You realise that your inhibitions were a construct of your mind. In your awareness of yourself, you start enjoying your own company; you enjoy listening to your own voice and thoughts.

My External Image Is Temporary and Breakable

My external image is nothing but my reflection in the water; even a tiny stone can send ripples through that. The world doesn't see me; it only sees a mirror in which I showcase the reflection of the best me. I show the world what I feel they need to see, but they never see the real me.

On the other hand, my awareness of myself is permanent, and it only improves and becomes stronger with time.

When you are more aware, your confidence increases since you are with the person who knows and understands you completely. Your productivity increases; you do not have to waste time on frivolous thoughts, which do more harm than you can imagine.

Once you are self-aware, the next step is to recondition your mind and thoughts towards positivity.

Now you may say that it is easier said than done, and you are not wrong. Self-awareness takes constant effort to be put into action. Once you have freed yourself from thoughts of others and your perception of opinions others have about you, you feel lighter and enjoy divine freedom. You are then at peace with yourself and your thoughts.

You will dress well out of your self-love, and you will speak well for your own listening pleasure. Self-awareness is not ego. Your awareness allows you to understand yourself, your strengths, and your weaknesses. Once you know yourself and are at peace with yourself, you will feel more content, you will make wiser decisions that are more in tune with your inner being.

Self-awareness is a journey; it is an ongoing process in which you keep learning something new about yourself. Your thoughts are then in line with your personality. This leads to actions that are more attuned to your personality, your real personality and not the image seen by the external world.

In my case, being a lawyer who quit a well-paying job in a top law firm very early on in my career to start my own law practice, I had a lot at stake. My fears were real. I had to prove myself to the world and especially to my father. That burden was heavy, and in that state, we make decisions not with awareness but as a necessity or at least a feeling of need.

So here I was, an IP lawyer taking up litigation matters, a non-contentious person taking up contentious matters. The number of litigation matters increased, and I kept taking them up out of my fears and ill-placed desires. Going against my authentic-self did take a toll on me. My stress levels were high, and I felt unhappy with what I was doing. Even though I was doing well professionally, I was ailing at a personal level. Contentious litigation was not easy for me at a personal level. The legal system compels you to twist and turn the facts, to scare and provoke, to implicate and entangle. My way of thinking did not check any of these boxes.

It was only when I decided to stop and examine why I was doing what I was doing that I became more aware of my default thinking and where it has led me. I decided to take charge. More control over my thoughts and emotions has led me to take control of my actions, which has helped me start the process of reshaping my life. I took tough decisions, which became possible only because I was aware of the reasons for those decisions. I had a purpose. The purpose was to take small steps to change my life's direction.

Now, the critical question that arises is how do we become self-aware. What are the steps, what is the process? As obvious as it may sound, the process starts with you. Certain personality traits are already wired into us, which are our tendencies. Although we can use meditation and affirmations to reprogramme some of those traits, however, that comes later.

What you need to do is to take small steps. We know many of our personality traits; we keep our true personalities wrapped up and packed up, but we are already aware of what's inside. So, next time you are making a decision you are feeling uncomfortable with, take a moment. Take a few deep breaths and question yourself whether the decision being taken is in line with your personality.

You cannot simply let go of a habit; you have to replace that habit with a more desirable one. Similarly, you cannot just stop your mind from thinking in a particular way. Still, with awareness, you can certainly teach it to think positive and clean thoughts that refresh and rejuvenate rather than negative thoughts that depress and damage.

Self-Awareness and Decision Making

There are no right or wrong decisions, just choices we make based on our thinking of what is right or wrong. That thought process results from our conditioning; it has been taught to us by our environment, parents, teachers, friends, classmates, and the rest of the world since birth.

Despite our upbringing, work requirements, and everything we do to survive the day, we feel uncomfortable when making certain decisions. Those are the decisions you will need to identify. Once you do that, you will need to introspect on why that decision made you uncomfortable. Does it go against your true nature?

The next question would be, what is your true nature? Am I living by my true nature? Am I taking this decision because it is suitable for me, or am I taking it because I am expected to take this decision?

These are difficult questions, and most of the time, the answer is not easy either. Moreover, it is not easy to change your decisions even when you become aware of what is eating you inside while taking that decision. Why, then, should you go through this additional burden? That is because it is the process that works.

The process starts with identifying the uncomfortable decisions, that tingling feeling that makes you tremble a little before deciding. Next, you need to take a step back to ask yourself the right questions. With time, you become aware of your true nature, what you really want, what your conscience allows, and what your consciousness really needs.

The next step is to start making difficult decisions, starting small. Most of our choices do not alter the course of our lives individually, but collectively they do. If you take small choices more in line with your personality, your true nature, eventually you will start taking all your decisions in this manner. As a result, you will feel more confident, happy, and your stress levels will go down.

Your decision-making will be faster, and you will be on your path to becoming a better leader.

In my journey, after making numerous small decisions, I eventually decided to quit taking up litigation matters, which took away half of my stress. My awareness of my being also allowed me to pursue things that I always wanted but could never surface earlier.

When I was young, I derived a lot of pleasure from writing. I wrote poems mostly, and each short poem felt like an achievement. However, my writing was written off since it was not considered a career, even though it may have been my calling. I could never know. In fact, when I dug through some of my old papers, I came across a poem I had written about twenty years back, and even at that time, when I was in my teens, I was unsure of what I was doing.

I took decisions only to please my parents. I had the need to feel that I was not letting them down. Now I realise that I cannot please others until I am of value in my own eyes. Until the time I am happy with myself, no matter what I do or did for others would never be good enough. Now I am 40, more in control of my life than I have ever been, and I realise how futile my steps had been, the decisions I took to please people around me.

Some lines from the poem I wrote more than twenty years ago are as follows:

I am not the one I used to be.
I am not the one I ought to be.
Still caught in the middle, unarmed.
Trying to get through this web unharmed.

The silence, then the winds of change,
I lie here waiting, my soul numb.
No words, no prayer, no homage to pay,
Wonder if I just live to sway.

...

Self-awareness gives you the confidence, boost, and positivity that allow you to believe in yourself, that enable you to embrace your true nature, and that help you realise your true worth.

Today, I am proud to say that I am doing everything that I love. I am following all my dreams and fulfilling my desires without any need for others' acceptance, admiration, or respect. I am achieving my true purpose one step at a time, enjoying that incomparable feeling of fulfilment and self-sufficiency. You can do that too. Just stop and listen to yourself whenever you feel uncomfortable and question yourself. Find the reason for being uncomfortable when making a decision, and the world will feel different from that moment onwards.

Conclusion

Self-awareness is the foundation of personal growth and transformation. It's the ongoing practice of turning our attention inward, of observing our thoughts, emotions, and patterns with curiosity and compassion. When we develop self-awareness, we gain the clarity and insight needed to make conscious choices aligned with our deepest values and aspirations.

One of the key components of self-awareness is mindfulness – the ability to be fully present in the moment without judgement. By regularly tuning into our inner experience, we can catch self-defeating patterns before they take hold, respond to challenges more skillfully, and make choices that truly nourish us.

Another crucial aspect of self-awareness is self-reflection. By taking time to regularly review our experiences, thoughts, and behaviours, we can extract valuable lessons and insights. We can identify our strengths, acknowledge our growth edges, and course-correct when necessary. Self-reflection allows us to continuously learn, adapt, and evolve.

Developing self-awareness also requires a willingness to embrace vulnerability. It means having the courage to honestly face our fears, insecurities, and blind spots. It means letting go of the need to be perfect and embracing our full humanity. Paradoxically, it's only by accepting ourselves as we are that we can create space for real change and growth.

A powerful tool for cultivating self-awareness is seeking feedback from others. By inviting trusted friends, family members, or colleagues to reflect on what they see, we gain invaluable mirrors for self-discovery. Others can often spot our patterns and potential in ways we can't see ourselves.

Ultimately, self-awareness is a lifelong journey, not a destination. It requires patience, self-compassion, and a commitment to continuous learning. It means being willing to peel back the layers of our conditioning and defences to uncover our authentic selves.

The benefits of self-awareness are profound. When we know ourselves deeply, we can communicate more effectively, build stronger relationships, and navigate life's challenges with greater resilience and grace. We can make choices that honour our truth and create a life that truly fulfils us.

Perhaps most importantly, self-awareness allows us to show up more fully for others. When we're not caught in our reactive patterns, we can be more present, compassionate and supportive of those around us. We can use our hard-earned wisdom to light the way for others.

The next time you find yourself on autopilot, take a moment to pause and turn your attention inward. Notice your breath, your feelings, and your inner dialogue. Approach whatever arises with kindness and curiosity. And remember that each moment of self-awareness is a gift, an opportunity to align your life with your deepest truth.

In the end, self-awareness is the key that unlocks our fullest potential. It's the path to authentic living, meaningful connection, and lasting fulfilment. By committing to the ongoing practice of knowing and honouring yourself, you set the stage for a life of incredible growth, depth, and purpose. And that is truly the greatest adventure of all.

Purpose of Life

Har ik ne apni raah banayi, har ik ne apna ghar basaya,
Kuch muddato mein phir chaley gaye, yahi faani duniya
ka maza hai.

– Mirza Ghalib (1797-1869)

Everyone created their own path, everyone built their own home,

But after a while, they all departed; that's the essence of this fleeting world.

What is the purpose of our life? That is one question that has been haunting me and many around me, maybe most of us, for a very long time. My search for the answer to this question has led me to much discontentment, disillusionment and disheartening times. With the lack of knowledge of my purpose, every action, every step in any direction was with a feeling of confusion and uncertainty. Whether this is part of my purpose? Am I moving in the right direction? Do I know what I am doing? In most cases, the answer would be, "I don't know," and with that answer, I had lost the battle before I even fought it.

I had prepared my mind to fail. Once that preparation has been made, it is hard to change your mind. Even a speck of doubt can make a mountain of difference. After much deliberation, I have understood that the purpose of life is to keep moving; the purpose of life is action, karma.

Remember: *Life's purpose is life's journey. The destination is irrelevant.*

I believe that as long as we are moving on any path, known or unknown, we are serving our purpose. If we are moving, we will keep taking different directions. Eventually, we will reach a road that we will relish moving on, and we may decide to keep moving on that road, a journey that we will cherish. Life's purpose is to keep moving, keep experiencing new paths. We will either find the path we will enjoy moving on or start enjoying the path we are moving on. We begin enjoying something either for the love of it or because we are adept at it due to extensive experience.

If you apply this concept to real-life scenarios, we can take any example of any facet of life. For example, let's take a career; suppose you are a software developer and have just landed your first job. Then you start thinking, is this why you have studied so much, just to sit in front of the screen and remotely troubleshoot systems of others? Then you have three options: (a) you can crib about it but keep on working in the same field; (b) you can change jobs, change careers, get further education, decide to move to another company, decide to move to another country, etc.; or (c) you can decide to quit everything and sit at home till some opportunity arises and falls in your lap.

If you choose the first option, you will, in time, find solace in your path. You will develop expertise, rise up the corporate ladder, become more confident in your field of work, and start enjoying the activities since you are now good at it.

If you choose the second option, you may feel disoriented and disillusioned at one point or another. Still, eventually, you reach a stage where you will feel that, yes, this is precisely what I was looking for, and you will keep moving on that path.

If you choose the third option, you are not going anywhere; you will never know what is in store.

Our destiny is karma. I do not believe in fate. You may, in your journey, have experiences where you feel lucky or unlucky. You come across such experiences only because you are moving forward. Take those experiences as learnings. Show gratitude to the universe and keep moving forward.

Assume that you have a physical problem, a minor physical problem such as a dandruff problem. What will you do? You cannot ignore it. You will feel embarrassed and irritated by the supposedly small issue. So, you will start searching for a treatment. You will buy some oil and try using it for a few days. If it doesn't work, you will try a new dandruff shampoo. You will find it is not too effective; then maybe you will try some Ayurvedic oil. If you find it a little better than the last product you used, you will keep using it. Then you will add some hair cream or hair tonic to the list of products you use. You will keep changing products and adding or subtracting treatments and products until you find the perfect combination. That is how you have to find your path, with trial and error, not by sitting down and waiting for the right product to show up on your doorstep. Opportunities do not conjure up; they are created.

As long as we are doing things and trying things, we will come across new people, and new experiences, which will enrich us and help us evolve. That, I believe, is the purpose of our lives.

Conclusion

The quest for purpose is a universal human journey. It's the deep yearning to understand why we're here, to find meaning in our existence, and to make a positive impact on the world around us. While the specifics of our individual purposes may vary, the search itself is a vital part of what makes us human.

One of the most powerful ways to uncover our purpose is to follow our curiosity and passion. When we engage in activities that light us up, time seems to disappear, and we feel a sense of flow and fulfilment. These are often clues to our deeper calling.

Another key to finding purpose is service to others. When we use our unique gifts and talents to make a difference in the lives of others, we tap into a wellspring of meaning and connection. We realise that our purpose is not just about us, but about the contribution we can make to the larger whole.

Purpose is also deeply linked to our values – the principles and ideals that guide our choices and actions. When we clarify what truly matters to us and align our lives accordingly, we naturally infuse our days with greater meaning and intention.

It's important to remember that our purpose is not a static destination, but an evolving journey. As we grow and change, so too does our understanding of why we're here. The key is to stay open and curious, to continuously explore new possibilities for expressing our unique gifts.

At the same time, finding purpose is not about grandiosity or perfection. It's about showing up authentically and doing what we can with what we have. It's about finding meaning in the small, everyday moments, as much as the big, life-changing ones.

Ultimately, the purpose of life is the purpose we give it. It's up to each of us to take responsibility for creating a life infused with meaning, joy, and service.

It's up to us to listen deeply to our own inner guidance and take courageous steps in the direction of our highest calling.

The irony is that when we focus on living purposefully, we often find that happiness and fulfilment come as natural byproducts. By losing ourselves in something larger than ourselves, we paradoxically find our truest selves.

The next time you find yourself wondering about your purpose, remember that the answer lies within you. Trust your intuition, follow your joy, and be willing to step into the unknown. Know that your unique journey is unfolding exactly as it's meant to, and that every experience is an opportunity to learn, grow and offer your gifts to the world.

The purpose of life is not a question to be answered, but a mystery to be lived. It's an ongoing invitation to explore, to create, to love, and to serve. By embracing that invitation with an open heart and a curious mind, we might just discover that the purpose of life is the one we create – one purposeful moment at a time.

Meditation

– Bhagavad Gita: Chapter 6, Verses 12-13

The yogi should sit firmly on the āsan (seat), making his mind focused. The yogi should control all the activities of his senses. The yogi should engage in meditation with one-pointed concentration for self-purification. He must remain motionless, holding the neck and head erect. His concentration should be on the tip of the nose, without wandering anywhere else.

If there is one thing that I would suggest and recommend for everyone to do more than anything else, it would be meditation. So if you read this book and forget about everything else written in this book, that is fine, as long as you remember this one thing, that meditation is essential for each of us.

Meditation is the act of connecting with oneself, your inner self, your consciousness. Once you are in touch with your inner being, the external influences will affect you less.

I noticed the value of meditation in April and May 2021, when the second wave of COVID-19 had engulfed the country. It was stressful with the external world going through turmoil not seen, heard, or experienced before. Everything and everyone around us seemed unreal. My meditation practice helped me stay calm.

Starting your meditation practice or your spiritual journey during turmoil is not an easy task. An adverse situation is when your practice of meditation and self-awareness comes into use. Only if you have been on that path already, then such obstacles will come and go. At the same time, the inner strength you would have gained will let you stay strong and stay on course, no matter how challenging the external situation. That is why the earlier you start, the better.

We have been taking our minds for granted for too long. Blessed are those who have experienced the powers and pleasures of meditation early on in life. They should feel lucky.

Meditation is an exercise for the brain. It has now been scientifically proven that it positively impacts the brain and re-energises your mind. Meditation calms you down, energises you, makes you conscious of your thoughts, and makes you self-aware.

It indirectly prevents you from negatively reacting to any adverse situation. It helps you maintain your balance when facing the most challenging situations in life, which lets you enjoy a fuller and peaceful life. An agitated mind will lead to wrong decisions. A calm mind will allow you to think logically and guide you to positive decision-making.

Reading about meditation can only help so much. When you know the benefits, you have to try it and practise it every day to reap its benefits. A word of caution, though, if you have not meditated before, your mind will fight. It has become comfortable in that noise; it will want you to stay the same. When we say we do not like change, it is not us but our mind talking. It likes the comfort of the known and avoids the unknown, no matter how beautiful the unknown might be.

There are several meditation techniques. You do not need to know all the methods, nor do you need to try each one to choose the one you like, though it is open for you to do that. Instead, you should start with a simple technique explained below, and if your curiosity leads you to try other methods, by all means, go ahead and try.

The Posture

- Sit down in a comfortable position with a straight back. Ideally, you should sit cross-legged. However, if that is not possible, you can sit on the side of your bed, chair, or sofa.

- Preferably, your hands should be in your lap, but depending on your sitting position, you may keep them on your thighs, lap, or the sidearm of your chair.
- Keep your shoulders proud, but not stiff.
- Keep your neck straight. It should follow the natural curve of your spine. If required, you may use a backrest, but do not use a headrest.
- Keep your teeth slightly apart. Our jaw holds a lot of tension. We clench our jaw when we are agitated or stressed. Keeping the jaw somewhat open immediately relaxes us.
- The tip of your tongue should touch your palate, just above the teeth.

The Technique

Start by taking a few deep breaths. Close your eyes. As you breathe, become aware of your body and the movement in your body. Notice the expansion and contraction in your chest and in your stomach. Bring your awareness to your ears and become aware of the sounds around you, such as the fan and the vehicles outside. As you become aware of the sounds, do not let those sounds start a train of thoughts. Observe, don't think. That means don't let your mind wander from one thing to the other. Acknowledge the movement in your body, take note of the sounds, and leave it at that.

The next step is to scan your body from head to toes by taking your awareness to each part of your body,

starting from the head. As you scan down, release any tightness you may feel in any part of your body. Loosen each body part as you scan them until your body is relaxed.

Next, bring your focus to the breath, to the inhalation and exhalation of breath. Keep your focus on the breath, and if your mind wanders, bring your attention back to the breath. Breathing is the object of this meditation. The reason is that our body does not need to put any effort into breathing. Breathing comes naturally, and we can bring back our attention to this natural process whenever our mind wanders.

Next, bring your attention to the nostrils. As you breathe, become aware of the sensations at the nostrils. The important thing is that you should bring your attention back to the breath every time your mind wanders. Initially, it may help to silently say "In-Out" or "Breathe in-Breathe out." However, this is not to be made a habit.

Counting

In the next step, we move to the process of counting. As you breathe in and breathe out, you count it as one. In this manner, count up to ten and then stop. Counting helps us focus on the object of our meditation, which is breathing. The counting is done up to ten since it is considered that our counting becomes mechanical after a point in time.

Now, just keep breathing and bring your attention back to breathing whenever your mind starts thinking or wandering. So, the idea is not to stop your mind from thinking, but to be aware of those thoughts and bring your attention back to breathing, and keep doing that for a few minutes.

Results

Now, this may not be a life-changing experience initially. But still, you will undoubtedly feel a little calmer than you were earlier. In fact, if you're feeling agitated or distressed for any reason, sit down and breathe in and out 5 to 10 times. You will immediately feel the difference in your mental make-up.

Also, when I initially started meditating, light meditation music helped, but it is optional. Try it and see if it enables you to focus better and prevent distractions; then you may include it in your routine. This can be helpful if you have too many distracting sounds around you.

Even if the noise in your head advises you against it, you make it a point to spend a few minutes with yourself daily, meditating. Do this at any time of the day or just before you go to bed at night. With time, you will observe palpable changes in your behaviour, your reactions, and your body language. You will witness positive changes in your thinking and your creativity. Embrace meditation, and you will start bringing positive change in your life.

I have heard people propound that meditation, mindfulness, and self-awareness only allow you to witness your thoughts. And to bring about change in your thinking, you are better off using affirmations and visualisations. I disagree with that. Can you really change something without identifying what needs to change and if it needs to change? To reach the stage of becoming an observer of your thoughts is an outstanding achievement and does not come easily. To be mindful and aware of your thinking, you have to be in a position to perceive them. That observation is a stage that comes with regular practice of meditation.

Until and unless I develop the power of witnessing my thoughts, the effects of my affirmations and visualisations will be short-lived. I am unlikely to see my reactions change when the time comes for my affirmations to kick in. If I am in a situation that is adverse to my personality, I would need my composure to be maintained and my confidence high to deal with the situation. What is the use of my affirmations if, at that time, I am unable to observe and mould my thoughts? If my current thinking carries me back to my old self, who would react with fear instead of the confidence I had wished to make part of my personality? I will be able to enhance my character only when I am observant of my thoughts. To change something, I need to know what really needs changing.

This is how I see it work:

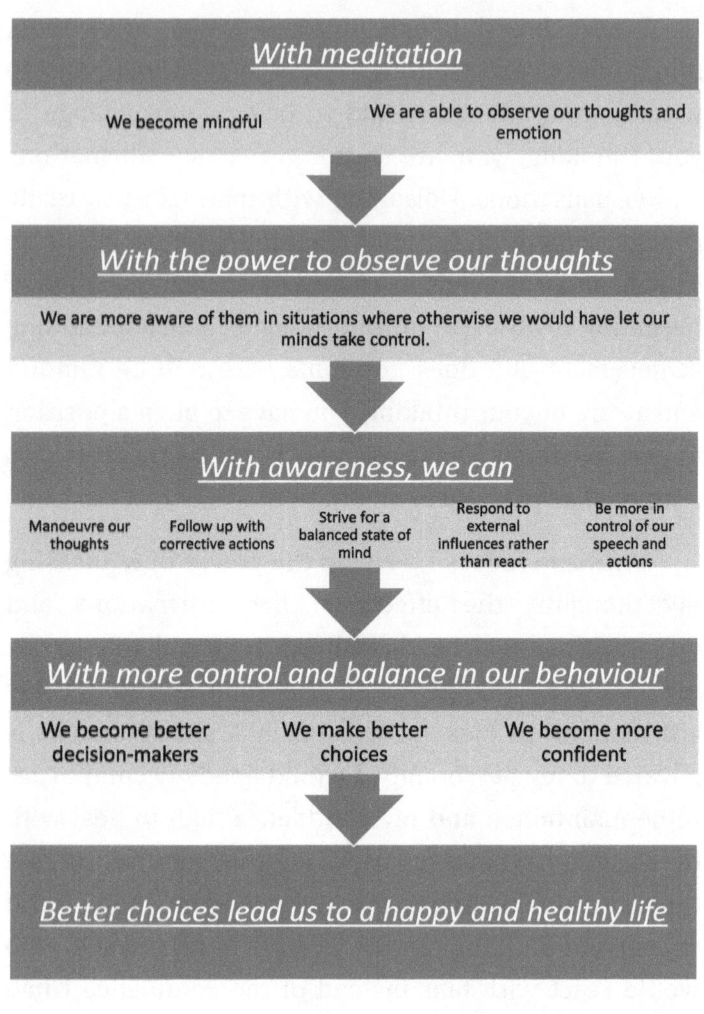

* * *

In his book, A Million Thoughts, Om Swami recommends holding a soft smile when you meditate. That simple change in posture will add immensely to your meditation results.

Just as the change in our mental make-up and our mindset can bring about a physical change in our external world, a change in our physical posture can bring about a mental change, a change in our inner world. This is because our mind and body are one, and when we meditate, we ask our mind and body to work as one.

You may have observed that when you are in bed, lying down, you feel lazy and sleepy; you can't work from there. Similarly, if you get up and sit at your study or work table, you will feel more alert and ready to study or work. That is because the physical or external change has led to a mental change, leading your mind to think differently. Similarly, when you add a smile while meditating, you will feel happier, more positive, content, and grateful when you are done with your meditation. This is the way to feel and be more abundant in your life.

Conclusion

Meditation is a transformative practice that has the power to profoundly impact every area of our lives. By taking time each day to sit in stillness and silence, we cultivate a deeper connection with ourselves, others, and the world around us. We tap into a wellspring of inner peace, clarity, and wisdom that can guide us through life's challenges and opportunities.

One of the greatest gifts of meditation is the ability to observe our thoughts and emotions without getting caught up in them. As we develop this capacity for mindful awareness, we create space between stimulus and response. We learn to respond to life's challenges with greater skill and equanimity, rather than reacting out of habit or impulse.

Meditation also helps us cultivate qualities like focus, resilience, and compassion. By training our minds to be present and attentive, we enhance our ability to concentrate and stay on task. By learning to sit with discomfort and uncertainty, we build the resilience to navigate change and adversity. And by practising loving-kindness and compassion, we deepen our capacity for empathy, connection, and service.

Perhaps most importantly, meditation helps us reconnect with our essential nature – the place of wholeness, peace, and joy that exists beyond our conditioned thoughts and beliefs. As we touch into this inner stillness, we remember who we truly are and what really matters.

It's important to approach meditation with patience, self-compassion, and an open mind. Like any skill, it takes practice and persistence to develop. The goal is not to stop our thoughts or achieve a particular state, but simply to show up consistently and do our best.

The beauty of meditation is that it meets us where we are. Whether we have one minute or one hour, whether we're feeling calm or anxious, whether we're new to the practice or seasoned meditators – every moment of mindful awareness counts. Each time we return to the present moment, we strengthen our capacity for presence and peace.

Ultimately, the fruits of meditation extend far beyond the cushion. As we integrate mindfulness into our daily lives, we naturally begin to live with greater intention, authenticity, and joy. We become more attuned to the beauty and possibilities in each moment. We show up more fully for ourselves and others.

The next time you find yourself caught up in the busyness and stress of daily life, remember the power of the pause. Take a moment to close your eyes, breathe deeply, and simply be. Trust that in the stillness and silence, you will find the guidance, resilience, and wisdom you need to navigate whatever life brings.

Meditation is a journey of self-discovery and self-mastery. It's a path of letting go and coming home. By committing to this path, one moment at a time, we open ourselves up to the profound peace, purpose, and potential that lie within. We remember that our deepest joy and fulfilment come not from changing our circumstances, but from changing our relationship to them. That is truly the greatest transformation of all.

Taking Control

Manzil milegi, bhatak kar hi sahi,
Gumarah to wo hain, jo ghar se nikle hi nahin.

– Mirza Ghalib (1797-1869)

You'll reach your destination, even if you wander, lost is the one who never even leaves home.

There is an enticement for taking the path that we can see clearly. It is comfortable and easier to go with the flow. We are but a drop of water in this big ocean. We do not want to make decisions that might create ripples in that ocean. We want to please everyone, keep everyone happy. So we go where the path takes us. If we question our own path, we feel stressed out, and to avoid that stress, we stop challenging ourselves, our way and our decisions. There are so many decisions that others would take for you or the world, in general, will take for you. You will follow the laid-out conventions; you will follow the path shown to you.

I am not saying that following the well-trodden path is wrong or deciding to follow that path is wrong. On the contrary, it is excellent as long as it was your own choice; it was a decision taken consciously out of your free will.

By going with the flow, I mean following a path not chosen by us but by others. A course decided for us without our say. How can I find purpose on a path I have not chosen for myself? There is no doubt that taking action is essential. It is the only thing that drives us to our purpose in life; however, if we are not following our own choices, if we are not following our own chosen path, in that case, it is possible, but unlikely, that we will reach a path we will find to be the path of our true calling.

How can that happen unless I am in control? I cannot be in control of my life if I am not in control of my decisions. And I cannot control my decisions if I live my life through the eyes of others.

When I make my decision, I have a responsibility to own up to my decision. Irrespective of the path's outcome, I will be satisfied since I will be rewarded one way or another, either through the desired results or through learning and experiencing. Such a path may lead to another path, and it will be open for me to take that next path. It will again be my decision to move onto the next track I see.

As long as I am making conscious choices, I am in control. When I have to make a decision, my mind will probe me. It will want me to weigh my options and consider all possibilities. Whatever the case, it will be my decision, and I will own it, learn from it, and be rewarded for it.

It is easier to blame others if it is just a path we are following, which is not of our choice. It is easier to allow others to make decisions for us. In that case, we have the option to blame others if the decision turns out to be wrong. We can shirk our responsibility for the consequences of the decisions taken by others. Also, our mind and body may not agree with the decision, but we may just follow it to avoid stress.

Since the responsibility of such a decision lies with someone else, we can become complacent and lax in our approach. As a result, we may not put in the right effort when treading on such a path. If, on the other hand, we are walking on a path of our choice, irrespective of whether the path will help accomplish our intended goal, we will put in more effort since we feel a sense of responsibility attached to our decision and a need to put in all our effort to satisfy that responsibility.

We may not be prepared and in a position to make our own decisions in our teens. We are dependent on our parents to show us the path, and more often than not, we end up following that path. Then, in our 20s, we explore the path we were sent on in a different setting, in the work environment. This is when it really settles in, when we get to know if we are on a path that resonates with us, with our consciousness, with our awareness of our own being.

You may also find yourself on a path that you enjoy, and you feel is perfect for you. In that case, be grateful and take control of your life from thereon.

When we are in our 30s, we have reached a stage where we have to own our decisions. When we have a choice to make whether to go with the flow and keep treading on the path chosen for us or take a turn, course-correct, towards another path we would have preferred if we were any wiser.

Whether I should get out of an unhappy marriage? Whether I should quit my job and start my own business? Whether I should disclose my sexual preferences to my parents? Whether I should quit my job and become an artist?

These questions are complicated, but they help us correct our course and set us out on the path of our choice, where we are in control and are ready to bear the consequences. So often, it's the path we are more scared to choose that we will take more control of. Now, no one can tell if the choice will be correct or not, or the results of that choice, but without any doubt, you will feel more satisfied and content on that path.

If your choice leads to a different path altogether and you feel scared and restless, you will need to prepare your mind and body before taking the leap. The best way to prepare yourself for the unknown and gain the strength to make your own decisions without any external influences, and be in control of your life, is through meditation.

Conclusion

Taking control of our lives is a courageous and empowering act. It means stepping out of the passenger seat and into the driver's seat of our existence. It means taking responsibility for our choices, our actions, and our outcomes. When we take control, we shift from being a victim of circumstance to being the creator of our reality.

One of the key aspects of taking control is developing a strong sense of personal agency – the belief that we have the power to influence our lives and make meaningful changes. This requires letting go of limiting beliefs, excuses and blame, and instead focusing on what we can do with what we have.

Another crucial component is setting clear intentions and goals. When we know where we want to go, we can create a roadmap to get there. We can break our big vision down into manageable steps and take consistent action towards our dreams. Each small step we take in the direction of our goals reinforces our sense of control and momentum.

Taking control also means being proactive rather than reactive. It means anticipating challenges and opportunities and taking deliberate steps to navigate them skillfully. It means being willing to have difficult conversations, make tough decisions, and take calculated risks in service of our values and aspirations.

At the same time, taking control doesn't mean controlling everything. It's about focusing on what we can influence and letting go of what we can't. It's about being adaptable and resilient in the face of change and uncertainty. It's about trusting ourselves to handle whatever arises with grace and wisdom.

Ultimately, taking control is about aligning our lives with our deepest truth and purpose. It's about creating a life that honours our unique gifts, passions, and values. It's about living authentically and wholeheartedly, even in the face of fear or resistance.

The irony is that when we take control of our inner world – our thoughts, beliefs, and responses – we naturally begin to influence our outer world in positive ways. We attract people, opportunities, and experiences that match our vibration. We create ripples of change that extend far beyond ourselves.

The next time you find yourself feeling stuck, powerless, or adrift, remember that you always have a choice. You can choose to take control of your mind, your actions, and your life. You can choose to step into your power and create the life you truly desire.

Taking control is not a one-time event, but a lifelong practice. It requires self-awareness, courage, and persistence. It means being willing to face our fears, learn from our mistakes, and keep showing up for ourselves and our dreams.

Taking control is about embracing our agency and authorship in this one wild and precious life. It's about recognising that while we may not control every circumstance, we always have the power to choose our response. And by consistently choosing to show up as the best version of ourselves, we create a life of incredible meaning, fulfilment, and impact. We become the heroes of our own story – and that is the greatest adventure of all.

Symbolism

Chinh hi chinh hai sara sansaar,
samajhne wala hi iska gyani

– **Swami Vivekananda, 19th century**
Hindu monk and philosopher.

The whole world is a collection of symbols; only the one who understands them is truly wise.

'Ganth Bandhna' is a Hindi phrase that some of you might have heard. It literally means 'Tying the knot' while its metaphorical meaning is 'To remember something completely'. I remember when I was very young, I saw a person tie the knot in her dupatta. I asked my mom what the reason for that was. "This is for her to remember something, a reminder of sorts," she told me. "The noticeable knot will remind her of whatever she doesn't want to forget. So she will find the knot in her dupatta and will be reminded of that thing or task," I was told.

I found the concept interesting but did not give it much importance. Eventually, when I reached the stage of needing reminders, I started using the good old pen and paper. I kept a small notepad in my pocket to remind myself of various tasks and quickly take down any notes. Then technology took over, and I started using to-do and reminder apps. Despite the apps, I still keep a small notepad since I do like the feel of putting pen to paper.

During my spiritual journey, I was reading, listening to, and trying new things. That is how I came across the chanting beads consisting of 108 beads strung together on a thread, used for chanting a mantra 108 times. Now, I never got used to chanting, but I kept the beads. While writing this, the chanting beads sit around my neck and remind me to follow the spiritual path. I have experienced the strength of that symbol in my life. It has helped me stay on course. Every time I stray in my thoughts or actions, just the touch or the look of those chanting beads helps me get back on track.

It was then that I remembered the proverb 'Ganth Bandhana' and the newfound use of it that I discovered. A symbol can be a constant reminder of the path you need to follow or of something you intend to change in your life. If it is on your person all the time, then you will be reminded of the course you are following at least a few times a day. And it will also help you stay on course.

If you decide to keep a reminder symbol, I suggest keeping an object that doesn't remind you of something or someone from your past. Your past is what you are trying to leave behind on your journey to a new and improved you. You do not want to be reminded of your past. You need to be forward-looking while you learn to live in the present. You need to have a way to visualise your future. A physical symbol could be a great way to remind you of the present, bring you back to the present whenever you go astray, and remind you of what you need to do in the present and the course you need to follow.

The symbol could be anything you can keep with you or wear to be reminded of your goal, purpose, or path every time you touch it, feel it, or look at it.

It should be something new. We do not want to live in the past; we do not want to be reminded of the past. Therefore, our symbol should bring us to the present, to the task at hand.

It should be something that can be changed once you have achieved a particular goal that the symbol reminded you of. If it is a life skill that the symbol represents, then you may keep it for longer. However, I would suggest getting a new symbol after some time. This is needed to bring in renewed energy into your symbol. Since, after some time has elapsed, seeing some kind of sign, which you have been looking at regularly, may become mechanical. It would not serve the purpose of a reminder. Once you feel that it has become such a part of you that you do not notice it, it is time to change it. So don't get yourself a permanent tattoo for this purpose.

Presently, I am using two such symbols. The chanting beads remind me to stay on my spiritual journey, and a toy car, which my three-year-old son graciously agreed to let me borrow, reminds me not to take life too seriously, to remain childlike, and to maintain that childlike innocence.

Symbols have been used since time immemorial. The power of symbolism has been used for generations since our forefathers understood the strengths of symbols. Symbols can represent many things. They can represent a faith, a religion, a brand name, a building, etc. Every time we see that symbol, such as a logo, we are reminded of that thing, faith, product, etc. If symbols have extraordinary powers, why can't we use them for something more profound and fruitful? I started using the symbols for a characteristic that I wanted to develop, change, or remind myself of something constantly. A small symbol can have a significant impact on our lives, and I recommend you try it to believe it.

Imagine yourself having negative thoughts about something. It could be anything someone has said, or it could be someone or something at your workplace, your home or a brush with road rage. Whatever it may be, imagine now that you have a symbol with you that has been with you or that you have been using for some time to develop optimism in your life, to remind you that life is not as bad as you may sometimes think. Now, once you already have that symbol with you, it will be easier for you to bring your negative thinking back to positive, the way you want it, and on which you have been working.

That one symbol of encouragement and affirmation is something I would suggest for everyone. It will help you live through the most difficult of times with strength and confidence.

You may have experienced that sometimes an object or even a smell can take you down memory lane because somewhere in your brain, that object or smell has a place that reminds you of some past instances. If a symbol can remind us of the past, we can also use its power to remind our brains of things we want to remember. This way, symbols can help us hack the programming of our brain and the conditioning of our mind.

Conclusion

Symbolism is the language of the soul, the secret code of the universe. It's the way our unconscious mind communicates profound truths and insights, the way the world around us mirrors our inner landscape. When we learn to recognise and interpret the symbols in our lives, we tap into a wellspring of wisdom, guidance, and transformation.

Symbols can take countless forms – from dreams and visions to signs and synchronicities, from art and literature to nature and everyday objects. Each symbol carries its own unique meaning and message, depending on the context and the individual. The key is to approach symbols with curiosity, openness, and a willingness to explore the deeper significance.

One of the most powerful ways to work with symbolism is through the practice of self-reflection and journaling. By recording and examining the symbols that appear in our lives, we gain invaluable insights into our unconscious patterns, beliefs, and desires. We can dialogue with our symbols, asking them what they have to teach us and how we can integrate their lessons.

Another potent tool is the use of creative expression. When we engage in activities like drawing, painting, writing, or storytelling, we give our symbols a tangible form and voice. We allow them to speak through us, revealing hidden aspects of ourselves and our world. The very act of creation becomes a symbolic ritual, a way of honouring and embodying the messages we receive.

Symbolism also connects us to the collective unconscious – the universal archetypes and themes that run through all human experience. When we encounter symbols that resonate deeply, we tap into a shared reservoir of meaning and mythology. We remember that our personal journey is part of a larger story, a timeless tapestry of human becoming.

Ultimately, symbolism is a gateway to the mystery and magic of existence. It reminds us that there is always more than meets the eye, that the visible world is just the tip of an infinite iceberg. By learning to read the symbolic language of life, we open ourselves up to a more enchanted, meaningful, and miraculous way of being.

The beauty of symbolism is that it meets us where we are and speaks to us in our own unique language. There is no right or wrong way to interpret a symbol, only the way that feels most true and resonant for us in the moment. The more we trust our intuition and follow the threads of our symbolic encounters, the more we weave ourselves into the larger web of meaning and purpose.

The next time a symbol catches your eye or tugs at your heart, pay attention. Pause and reflect on what it might be trying to communicate. Allow yourself to be drawn into the deeper conversation, the one that takes place beneath the surface of everyday reality. Trust that the symbols that appear in your life are not random or meaningless, but are sacred signposts guiding you home to yourself.

Symbolism is an invitation to live a more aligned, authentic, and awakened life. It's a reminder that we are not just human beings having a spiritual experience, but spiritual beings having a human experience. By learning to read the symbolic language of the soul, we remember our place in the grand tapestry of creation. We become co-creators of our reality, weaving our unique thread of meaning and magic into the great mystery of existence.

Spirituality

Īśā vāsyam idam sarvam yatkiñca jagatyām jagat

- Isha Upanishad (Verse 1)

All that exists in the universe is pervaded by the Divine.

Spirituality is the knowledge that you are more than just your physical body. Once you internalise this knowledge and accept it as the ultimate truth, you feel empowered. This knowledge allows you to let go of your ego. The world will go on, with or without you, and if you look inside, you will find the whole world within you.

Spirit is the life energy within you. This life energy is not separate from the source energy that created you and created the universe. You can call this source energy by different names. You can call it God, the Infinite Intelligence, the Divine Force, the Life Source, etc. The truth is that since we are part of the source energy, we are not different from nature. We are a part of nature; we are nature itself.

Owing to the life energy within us, we are connected with all other living creatures on this planet and beyond. Spirituality is the knowledge that we are a combination of our mind, body, and spirit. When we delve deeper and realise that the scientific understanding of mind and body alone cannot fully explain our being, we are on our spiritual journey.

A spiritual journey is a process of acknowledging our spiritual self, the part of our being that science hasn't discovered yet and can only be felt by us. This life energy is both a creator and a destroyer. With positive thoughts, we create, and with negative thoughts, we destroy. Our thoughts are the fuel for this energy. We can either direct our thoughts towards creation or towards destruction. Energy itself can neither be created nor destroyed. It can only be transformed from one form to another. Just like mechanical energy can be converted into electrical energy, negative and positive energies we create with our thoughts will also change form and create negative and positive environments. The energies will run in the direction we show them. We can choose to live a life with the awareness of our spiritual beings or let life play out on its own without awareness. The choice is ours.

However, suppose we do start becoming aware of our self, our spirit, our life energy. In that case, we can start looking at everything around us with a more detached outlook. That does not mean that we lose interest in life. In fact, life becomes more interesting, since we start to realise and feel that we are all connected.

The feeling of detachment allows us to look at life more clearly. We can observe our thoughts objectively.

It will enable us to understand the 'why' instead of only seeing the 'what' in everything around us. For example, instead of asking, "What am I doing?" you will start asking, "Why am I doing this?" Being spiritual also does not prevent us from action. In fact, it pushes us to do more since we can look at situations and people not under the shadow of emotions, but with detachment.

We are spiritual when we connect with our inner being. We are spiritual when we realise the divine nature of our being. We are spiritual when we accept that we are more than our physical bodies. We start to acknowledge that powers beyond our present understanding are around us. We realise that we are filled with creative energies, which can be constructive or destructive, depending on whether those energies are directed or misdirected.

You awaken to your spiritual self when you start paying attention to it. For some people, this happens on its own. For others, it is triggered by a life event such as going through a tragic event like the death of a loved one. For the rest, it never happens. Therefore, you must surround yourself with the proper knowledge and the right people. Surround yourself with everything that empowers you. Spend some time in silence, preferably in places where you can connect with nature, maybe a park or a garden. Sit back and observe the natural surroundings around you. Let your mind wander on the wondrous nature and acknowledge the miracle of life. Human beings can be as complex and as simple as you take them to be. See yourself as nothing short of a miracle.

You are a miracle of nature. Everything we need is provided by nature. So let nature be your guide. Open your heart to nature, to your Source Energy, to your Divine Creator. Over time, your worldview will change, your perception will change, your perspective will change. We are all connected by nature. Once your consciousness becomes aware of such connections, you will start to feel that connection and start looking for them. It gives that feeling of contentment and satisfaction that we feel when we are sitting or walking in the park or forest.

Conclusion

Spirituality is the journey of the soul, the quest for meaning, purpose, and connection beyond the material world. It's the recognition that we are more than our physical bodies, our thoughts, or our circumstances – that we are eternal beings having a temporary human experience. When we embark on the spiritual path, we open ourselves up to a deeper understanding of ourselves, others, and the universe at large.

One of the core aspects of spirituality is the cultivation of a personal relationship with the divine; however, we choose to define it. Whether we call it God, Spirit, Higher Power, or simply the essence of love and wisdom, connecting with this larger presence can provide a profound sense of guidance, support, and belonging. It reminds us that we are never truly alone and that there is a benevolent force at work in our lives.

Another key element of spirituality is the practice of inner exploration and self-discovery. Through techniques like meditation, prayer, contemplation, and self-inquiry, we turn our attention inward and begin to uncover the layers of our being. We confront our shadows, heal our wounds, and reconnect with our authentic selves. We learn to listen to the whispers of our soul and align our lives with our deepest truth.

Spirituality also invites us to see the inter-connectedness of all things – to recognise that we are part of a vast web of life, each thread interwoven with every other. As we cultivate this awareness, we naturally develop greater compassion, empathy, and reverence for all beings. We feel called to live in greater harmony with ourselves, others, and the planet as a whole.

Ultimately, spirituality is about transcendence – rising above the limitations of the ego and connecting with something greater than ourselves. It's about recognising that our true nature is boundless, eternal, and infinitely creative. As we awaken to this truth, we begin to live from a place of surrender, trust, and flow. We become channels for divine love and wisdom to pour through us.

The beauty of spirituality is that it is a highly personal journey, unique to each individual. There is no single right path, only the one that resonates most deeply with our own heart and soul. Some may find their spirituality through religious tradition, others through nature, art, or service. The key is to follow our own inner compass and trust the unfolding of our journey.

At the same time, spirituality is not about bypassing the challenges and responsibilities of the material world. Rather, it's about bringing a heightened awareness and presence to every aspect of our lives. It's about infusing our relationships, work, and daily actions with a sense of meaning, purpose, and sacred connection.

The next time you feel the call of your soul, the tug of something greater, trust it. Allow yourself to be drawn into the mystery and the wonder of existence. Know that your spiritual journey is unfolding exactly as it's meant to and that every experience is an opportunity to deepen your connection to yourself, others, and the divine.

Spirituality is the greatest adventure of all – the journey home to our true selves. It's the recognition that we are not here by accident, but by divine appointment. That we each have a unique role to play in the great unfolding of consciousness. And that by embracing our spiritual nature, we tap into a wellspring of love, wisdom, and creative power that can transform our lives and our world. May we each have the courage and the grace to answer the call of our soul and embark on this sacred journey with an open heart and a curious mind.

Mental Health

Sukh duhkh do pahariya, rain din baraat jaat.
Man changa to kathin kaam bhee sukhadaayak hot.

– Kabir Das (15th-century mystic poet)

Suffering and happiness are like two wheels. Night and day pass by like this.

If the mind is pure, even difficult tasks become enjoyable.

They are among us: family, friends, colleagues, whose pain cannot be seen but felt. Mental health issues have become more common than ever. Internal pain that a person is suffering manifests as an external change in behaviour.

As an outsider, it is difficult for us to understand what might trigger depression in someone. What may seem trivial to one person might be the biggest challenge faced by another. Everyone is on their individual journey, and every person gets to decide what might be essential for them.

I have seen amiable and socially active people disconnect from the outside world and go into their cocoons, where they are surrounded by their own thoughts. Unfortunately, those are not positive thoughts. To another person, it may seem that such a person is attracted to pain and suffering as if the person enjoys being in pain. That, of course, is not the case. Physical pain can be seen by others, and your loved ones are around to help you with that. Mental pain is internal, and a person suffering feels that nobody sees or knows their pain. They think they don't have anybody for support and that they are alone. This feeling of being forsaken increases the intensity of pain. Eventually, it sinks deep into the person to the extent that it becomes difficult to let go of that feeling.

By the time this pain shows outside with unexplained behavioural changes, depression would have strengthened its hold on the person. Our relationship with internal pain and suffering does not evolve; it is the same for a child who lost her favourite toy and an adult who lost a loved one. Our ability to deal with such pain changes and evolves as we grow. Our needs and priorities change. What might be valuable at 13 may be irrelevant at 33.

Unfortunately, we have not been taught about dealing with pain. We may have compassionate, loving people around us, which will positively impact our external environment, but if the pain is inside, we need tools within us to overcome that pain. The four steps for dealing with internal pain are:

- Acceptance
- Seeking help
- Empowerment
- Overcoming

Acceptance

The first step is to accept the problem. Our society has made it very difficult for us to admit to suffering. If we are asked how we are doing, we mechanically answer that we are well and fine. Being in pain is seen as a sign of weakness, and our society does not forgive the weak. It does not discourage trampling over the weak. Unfortunately, sometimes, even empathy and compassion are seen as signs of weakness. Parents don't have time in the cutthroat world we live in. Most schools are mechanical in their approach. They have to confine themselves to a set syllabus, which unfortunately does not consider value education a subject of any relevance. In such an environment, how could someone admit that they are in pain? The person does feel weak and doesn't know what to do, and they do not realise that they need support.

The long-term game plan should teach our kids that it is okay to be afraid, sad, or anxious. But, more importantly, we need to teach our children the importance of understanding and accepting their feelings. Once we accept a certain feeling, once we are no longer ashamed of being afraid or anxious, we will develop the tools, the antibodies, to overcome those feelings. If you are not equipped to handle a bad feeling, it will thrive inside us like a virus.

The first and most crucial step is to accept. The earlier we accept, the easier it would be for us to start the healing process.

Sometimes, people around a person will realise that they are going through internal suffering. In such a situation, it may not be wise to announce your judgement to the person suffering. The best course, in my opinion, would be to ensure, with words and actions, that they realise they have people in their life who are there to support and help. If the external environment is conducive, it will be easy for the person suffering to understand that their pain is internal, since the external environment is not presenting anything that will cause them pain. That may lead to such an individual accepting the presence of a feeling that is not a result of their outside world.

Accepting a problem is half the battle won. If you avoid confronting a problem, you are only adding fuel to the fire. Problems will not mend themselves on their own. Avoiding a problem does not make it go away. It only makes it stronger.

Add the following affirmation to your routine:

I cannot control my environment and my surroundings most of the time. But, I am the master of my feelings, and I can control and manoeuvre my feelings.

Seeking Help

Once you have accepted that your mental health needs improvement, the next step is to seek some help to do that. Start by revealing your feelings to a confidant. This could be your spouse, parent, or friend. Any person you feel comfortable sharing your feelings with, a person you trust, can be your confidant. It will be better if the person is a good listener since, at this time, you would only be looking to offload what's on your mind and not expect the other person to start giving you solutions.

When you reveal all this information to a confidant who will listen to you about your fears, thoughts, and feelings non-judgementally, you will instantly feel relaxed and lighter.

Depending on the severity, you may need medical help and assistance. If that is the case, do not be apprehensive or afraid of doing that. You need to understand that it is an illness that needs to be treated just like any other illness. Why do doctors, psychologists, and psychiatrists have to study so much about treating mental conditions? That is because there is so much to learn. That means there has been so much research in the field for such a long time. My point being, you are not the only one suffering from a mental health issue. It might feel like that since your thoughts and feelings make you believe in that negative construct of the mind. It may seem that everyone else is happy and content, living their lives, not having any problems in their lives. You will, of course, be wrong in reaching that conclusion.

Despite how they may seem to the outside world, most people are only trying to take their own little steps and actions to reach a stage where they may feel happy and stay happy. But, unfortunately, as I have said before, such a state of being is not possible until you are looking for happiness externally rather than internally. To look inward, you will have to be brave enough to face your inner fears and negative thoughts.

If you are in a mental state where you cannot do it independently, you may need help from your confidant and your doctors. So, do not be afraid to seek help; do not feel less for having to receive support. Life will reward you with all its glory as long as you allow it.

Empowerment

Having accepted that there exists a problem also develops a desire to overcome that problem. The will to overcome may need strengthening over time. However, one method allows you to reinforce your way to come out of adverse situations. That is the method of taking constructive action. That constructive action could be anything that lets you be creative. It could be a hobby, developing a new website, a business, an artwork, a research paper, volunteering at a charity organisation, or being actively involved in your Resident Welfare

Association; anything under the sun that implores you to create.

All of us are creative by design, and most of us are non-creative by default. Our environment may have prevented us from showcasing creativity. Still, just like necessity is the mother of invention, affliction is the motivation for novelty.

If you would try to remember all the times in your life when you have felt satisfied, content, and happy, you would discover that most of these times are when you have created something. We are on this Earth to create. Our creations help us live better and, in the process, help others around us live better lives. Therefore, when we find ourselves in a situation where negative thoughts have overtaken our minds, we can start the process of reversing our thought process by indulging ourselves in constructive and creative work.

When you build or create something, you feel empowered, which is the feeling that is cherished and is a feeling that tides over the negative thoughts that might be bringing you down, making you feel disempowered and helpless.

Along with engaging in something creative and constructive, indulge in some physical activity, be it a sport or exercise. Physical activity relieves mental stress. In addition, the endorphins and dopamine released in your body will provide a boost to help rid you of your mental troubles.

Overcoming

Everything external is short-lived and momentary. For long-lasting positive results, you have to look inside. If you are looking for happiness, you will need to find it inside. If you are looking for love, you need to love yourself first. If you are looking for motivation, you will need to find it inside. If you're looking to overcome fears and negativity, you will need to empower yourself from the inside.

External solutions can support you but can never replace the true happiness, love, motivation, and power within you. To enable that inner power, you will have to use meditation and affirmations. Meditation is not easy with a troubled mind. It is a process that works when your mind is in a calm state. Regular practice helps you develop mental toughness, which helps ward off inner turmoil when the external circumstances are difficult. The practice takes over when the situation so requires, but initiating the practice of meditation when you are already in a challenging situation, internally or externally, may not be possible. If meditation seems difficult initially, start with affirmations, resolving to be happy, joyous, and empowered, and soon those feelings will take centre stage in your mind, replacing the negative thoughts and emotions that were preventing you from being your true self, from being the creator that you are meant to be. When the mind is calmer, start a meditation routine.

Conclusion

Mental health is an essential component of our overall well-being, just as vital as our physical health. It encompasses our emotional, psychological, and social well-being and impacts how we think, feel, and act in our daily lives. When we prioritise our mental health, we create a foundation of resilience, adaptability, and vitality that allows us to navigate life's challenges and opportunities with greater ease and joy.

One of the key aspects of maintaining good mental health is self-awareness – the ability to recognise and understand our own thoughts, feelings, and behaviours. By developing this inner attunement, we can catch early warning signs of distress and take proactive steps to care for ourselves. We learn to identify our triggers, set healthy boundaries, and communicate our needs effectively.

Another crucial component is self-care – the practice of nurturing ourselves on all levels: physically, emotionally, mentally, and spiritually. This can include activities like regular exercise, healthy eating, sufficient sleep, creative expression, social connection, and mindfulness practices. By making self-care a priority, we replenish our reserves, boost our mood, and enhance our overall resilience.

Mental health also involves developing a toolkit of healthy coping strategies for managing stress, anxiety, and difficult emotions. This can include techniques like deep breathing, progressive muscle relaxation, journaling, cognitive reframing, and seeking support from others. The more tools we have at our disposal, the more equipped we are to handle life's inevitable ups and downs.

It's important to remember that mental health exists on a continuum, and that we all face challenges and struggles at times. Seeking help when needed is a sign of strength, not weakness. Whether it's reaching out to a trusted friend, joining a support group, or working with a mental health professional, getting the support we need is a crucial part of maintaining our well-being.

Ultimately, prioritising our mental health is about choosing to live fully, authentically, and joyfully. It's about honouring our own unique needs, desires, and boundaries. It's about cultivating a loving and compassionate relationship with ourselves so that we can show up more fully for others and the world around us.

The beauty of mental health is that it is a practice, a journey, not a destination. Each day presents new opportunities to check in with ourselves, make nourishing choices, and course-correct when needed. The more we prioritise our mental well-being, the more we naturally align with our deepest values and highest potential.

The next time you find yourself struggling, remember that you are not alone and that there is always hope and help available. Reach out, speak up, and trust that you have the inner resources and outer support to navigate whatever challenges arise. Know that by caring for your own mental health, you are not only transforming your own life but also contributing to a more compassionate and resilient world.

Mental health is about embracing our full humanity – our light and our shadow, our strengths and our vulnerabilities. It's about learning to dance with the full spectrum of our experience and finding meaning, purpose, and connection along the way. By making mental health a priority, we not only enhance our own lives but also create ripples of positive change that extend far beyond ourselves. May we each have the courage, compassion, and commitment to nurture our own mental well-being and to support others in doing the same. For in caring for our minds, we heal our world, one heart at a time.

Part 2

Outer Reboot

Experiences

If you can make one heap of all your winnings
And risk it on one turn of pitch-and-toss,
And lose, and start again at your beginnings
And never breathe a word about your loss;
If you can force your heart and nerve and sinew
To serve your turn long after they are gone,
And so hold on when there is nothing in you
Except the Will which says to them: "Hold on"

...

Yours is the Earth and everything that's in it,
And – which is more – you'll be a Man, my son!

From 'If—' by Rudyard Kipling

One thing to always remember is that there are no mistakes in life, only experiences. Those experiences may or may not be good experiences, but all of them have one thing in common: learnings. Our task and endeavour should be to use those experiences and find the path that the universe has paved for us. The universe is waiting for us to discover that path; we only need to keep our minds open and keep moving forward. You will find your way, but only if you are looking for it. It is easy to keep wandering wherever life takes us, and it takes courage and awareness to go towards our calling, where the universe wants you to be, where your soul wants you to go.

Life is a journey of experiences, a stream of experiences. Each and every encounter with the world is an experience. That encounter could be good or bad, and the experience that ensues could similarly be good or bad. But one thing is for sure, that all experiences are learnings which we should cherish.

As we grow, we start developing a certain rigidity that prevents us from trying new things. Conversely, being flexible allows us to enrich our experiences. The reason for this rigidity and our need for predictability is our fear of the unknown and our fear of failure.

Without new experiences, the journey of life becomes listless and dull. Routine is comfortable, but to achieve anything, you need to come out of that comfort zone. Too much comfort could make you predictable. To be good, life does not need to be predictable. Predictability is required only in your belief system, which should be one of faith, joy, compassion, cooperation, and gratitude. Other than that, the excitement in your life is inversely proportional to the predictability in your life. The more predictable it is, the less stimulating it will be, and vice versa. Novelty challenges us and excites us. We do not need to turn into shrewd or cunning persons to experience newness.

To find our path, our calling, that place on Earth that belongs to us, we will need to overcome our fears. Life is a journey of self-discovery. Our fears and worries prevent us from treading on that journey. We sell ourselves short, and we hope that our life's purpose will be laid down for us by others or by our destiny. We hope that it will appear out of nowhere, and then we will start to live our life like we are supposed to. Most of us end up spending our life waiting for life's big plan to be revealed to us. When we do not see any indication of such revelation, we start cursing our environment, childhood, school, parents, spouse, and children; everything, except ourselves, for not getting to live the life we desired. Desires are ours, but we make everything and everybody else the medium for fulfilling those desires.

Two people can go to the same restaurant on the same day and have opposite experiences. The restaurant is the same, the chef is the same, the staff is the same, yet two people experience the place differently. One person will praise the restaurant while the other will blame the restaurant, the staff, the chef, the manager, etc., for having ruined the day. Will this terrible experience stop this person from visiting any other restaurant? No. Does having had a bad experience once mean that all restaurant experiences would be poor? No.

The truth is that life is an individualistic experience. My experiences are my truth, and that may not be true for you. Why, then, should we stop ourselves from experiencing more in life? Why should we stop ourselves from new experiences? Why should we blame others for our bad experiences? The only hurdle that we need to overcome to experience life to the fullest is fear.

Conclusion

Experiences are the currency of a rich and meaningful life. They are the moments that shape us, the stories we tell, the memories we cherish. When we prioritise experiences over material possessions, we invest in our growth, connection, and fulfilment. We recognise that the true value of life lies not in what we have, but in who we become through what we live.

One of the greatest gifts of embracing a life of experiences is the opportunity for continuous learning and expansion. Each new experience, whether travelling to a foreign country, taking up a new hobby, or having a deep conversation with a stranger, offers us a chance to step outside our comfort zone and broaden our perspective. We learn to see the world, and ourselves, through new eyes.

Experiences also have the power to connect us more deeply to others and to the world around us. When we share an experience with someone, whether it's a friend, family member, or even a brief encounter, we create a bond that transcends the superficial. We tap into our common humanity and the universal joys and challenges of being alive. We remember that we are all in this together.

Moreover, experiences have a way of bringing us into the present moment like nothing else. When we are fully engaged in an activity, whether hiking a mountain trail, creating a piece of art, or savouring a delicious meal, our worries and distractions fade away. We become absorbed in the richness of the here and now. We taste the fullness of life in all its flavours.

It's important to note that meaningful experiences don't have to be grand or exotic. Some of the most profound moments can be found in the ordinary magic of daily life – a heartfelt conversation with a loved one, a quiet moment of self-reflection, a gesture of kindness to a stranger. The key is to approach each moment with a sense of openness, curiosity and presence.

Ultimately, a life rich in experiences is a life well-lived. It's a life of courage, connection, and continuous becoming. It's a life that recognises that our time here is finite and that each moment is an opportunity to learn, grow, and make a positive impact.

The beauty of prioritising experiences is that it's never too late to start. No matter our age, background, or circumstances, we can always choose to embrace new adventures, to step out of our routines, and to say yes to the call of life. Each new experience is a chance to reinvent ourselves, to discover new aspects of our being, and to fall in love with life all over again.

The next time you find yourself at a crossroads, choosing between an experience and a possession, remember the true wealth that experiences offer. Choose the path that expands your horizons, nourishes your soul, and connects you more deeply to yourself and others. Trust that by living a life rich in experiences, you are creating a masterpiece of moments that will shape you and inspire others for years to come.

Experiences are the true essence of a life well-lived. They are the brushstrokes of our unique story, the colours of our ever-evolving canvas. By embracing a life of experiences, we not only enrich our journey but also contribute to the collective tapestry of human becoming. May we each have the courage and the openness to say yes to the adventure of life and to create a legacy of experiences that will forever remind us of the beauty and the brevity of our time here on Earth.

Fear of Missing Out

We have already discussed the fears that grip us internally and stop us from being our real selves. It is also important to discuss another fear that has gripped our generation and is responsible, among other factors, for many of our problems, including low self-esteem, avoiding social interactions, anxiety, and depression. That is the fear of missing out, or FOMO as it is more commonly known.

This fear is the direct result of one of our generation's most significant achievements: the internet. With access to so much information and content, an average person is bound to be overwhelmed every day. The result is that you may feel the need to consume as much data, information, and content lest you miss out on something seemingly relevant. It could be as menial as a new show on Netflix, a topic of discussion among your friends and peers, a stock whose share price took a short-term dip, a piece of news, or any other thing under the sun.

It is normal to have that fear to some extent. However, if it leads to symptoms of physical or mental anxiety or drives you down the path of becoming an internet junkie, you need to take action.

I was so fixated on keeping track of the news that I ended up checking news apps every thirty minutes. I had taken myself off social media for a few years, yet I had the urge to keep track of content and news every hour. I would just open the news app and go through the news stream. What purpose did that serve? I can't think of any except that I could more passionately discuss the news piece among my colleagues or friends. The next day, news changed, the topic changed, discussions kept going on.

After wasting several precious hours, I realised that 99% of the information I was bingeing on was junk. With services like YouTube churning out thousands of hours of content every minute, you can spend a lifetime consuming information without even scratching the surface.

If you are stuck in that rut too or ever find yourself stuck in such a scenario, you will need to take a step back. There is no magic formula for anything in life, but taking steps in the right direction is essential for your own sake.

I have applied some principles to myself and have seen positive results, such as:

- Meditation,
- Slowing down, reflecting, and taking my time
- Digital detoxification,

Try to remember what content you consumed last week, be it information, data, news or video content. You will realise that you have forgotten most, if not all, of it. Next, think about what information was of actual relevance. You will realise that only a minuscule amount is useful and worth knowing; the rest is just junk.

Go back to the old ways, pick up a book to read to keep your mind occupied. Instead of opening up a news app, just pick up the newspaper for your daily dose of current affairs. The world does not change in a few hours. Until that happens, relax and enjoy being in the moment.

Add the following affirmations to your daily routine:

I am in control

I am spending my time wisely.

I think we should now start replacing FOMO with JOMO, the Joy of Missing Out. Wouldn't we be better off without most of the information and content we come across these days? How much of that information really affects us? That question is easy to answer; just try to remember how much of the content or information from just two days ago. 99% of the information received is already forgotten. No wonder our attention span has drastically reduced over the last decade or so.

Conclusion

The Fear of Missing Out, or FOMO, has become a pervasive phenomenon in our modern, hyper-connected world. It's the nagging feeling that everyone else is living a more exciting, fulfilling life than we are and that by not participating in every social event, career opportunity, or life experience, we are somehow falling behind. But while FOMO may be a common experience, it's important to recognise its detrimental effects on our mental health, relationships, and overall quality of life.

At its core, FOMO stems from a place of scarcity and comparison. It's the belief that there's not enough to go around – not enough time, not enough opportunities, not enough happiness. It's the constant measuring of our own lives against the curated highlight reels of others. But when we buy into this mindset, we rob ourselves of the joy and contentment of the present moment. We miss out on the depth and meaning that comes from fully engaging with what's in front of us.

The antidote to FOMO is JOMO – the Joy of Missing Out. It's the radical acceptance that we cannot do and be everything, and that that's okay. It's the recognition that by saying no to certain things, we are saying a deeper yes to what truly matters to us. It's the understanding that a life well-lived is not about the quantity of our experiences, but the quality of our presence and engagement.

Cultivating JOMO requires a shift in perspective and priorities. It means getting clear on our values and boundaries and making choices that align with them. It means practising gratitude for what we have, rather than fixating on what we lack. It means investing in the relationships and pursuits that truly nourish us, rather than spreading ourselves thin trying to keep up with everyone else.

Another key aspect of overcoming FOMO is developing a healthy relationship with technology and social media. While these tools can connect us in powerful ways, they can also fuel feelings of inadequacy and disconnection when used mindlessly. By setting intentional limits on our screen time, curating our online experiences to support our well-being, and regularly unplugging to be fully present in the real-world, we can break free from the FOMO cycle.

Ultimately, releasing FOMO is about embracing the truth that we are each on our unique path and that there is no one-size-fits-all blueprint for a meaningful life. It's about learning to trust our inner compass and having the courage to follow it, even when it leads us away from the crowd. It's about defining success and happiness on our terms rather than society's expectations.

The beauty of letting go of FOMO is that it frees up so much energy and attention for what really matters. When we stop chasing after an idealised version of life, we can start savouring the imperfect beauty of the one we have. We can cultivate deeper relationships, pursue our passions with greater focus, and find peace in the stillness between the big moments.

The next time you feel the pull of FOMO, remember that you have a choice. You can buy into the scarcity mindset and exhaust yourself trying to keep up, or you can choose the abundant path of JOMO. You can recognise that every yes is a no to something else and that that's not only okay but necessary for a life of purpose and balance.

Overcoming FOMO is about reclaiming our power to choose how we spend our time and energy. It's about having the discernment to know what truly enriches our lives and the discipline to prioritise those things above all else. By embracing JOMO, we open ourselves up to a life of greater depth, meaning, and true fulfilment – not despite what we're missing, but because of it. And that is the greatest adventure of all.

Time

sadā aish daurāñ dikhātā nahīñ
gayā vaqt phir haath aatā nahīñ

– Meer Hasan

The course of time does not always show pleasures,

Time lost does not come back into hands again

If there is one perishable commodity that is the be-all and end-all of everything in life, it is time. In my thirties, I realised its actual value and how quickly it could fly. I think everyone would have heard from their parents about the importance of time and how valuable it is.

I would go on to say that it is the most precious commodity we have been bestowed with, and it is our duty and, in our own best interest, to spend it wisely.

In our teens, we do not really think about time. We are busy dealing with school, puberty, and career choices. Therefore, time does not feature in our list of priorities since we feel we have lots of it.

In our twenties, we are just stepping out into the world from the cocoons our parents built around us for safety from the world we now need to face. We are busy working on our careers and professions. It is a new start, and who will think about the end when we are just starting out.

The twenties go by quickly while we work on establishing ourselves in our careers. Many of us get married in our twenties, so there are a lot of new starts. Time is of least importance when you start new things, since we think we are in for a long haul. As a result, contemplating the importance of time takes a back seat. We will still be running short of time for our deadlines, but a broad understanding of the limited time of our life on Earth is absent.

Many of us find ourselves settled into most aspects of our lives in our thirties, be it career or marriage. I am not saying that all of us are happy with our profession or marriage, but the novelty has worn off by now, and we can see things for what they are. Our perspective changes. Now, our mind starts calculating the time we have left to do things we want to do, something we had always wished to do.

It was only in my mid-thirties that it dawned on me that time was running out. Sometimes, our circumstances can trigger such feelings. For example, losing a family member can remind us of our mortality and the need to use our time on Earth, not abuse or misuse it.

Death is life's great leveller. We know we are not immortals. Reminding ourselves, every once in a while, that we have limited time on Earth helps us rethink our priorities and arrive at our purpose. When we know that we have limited time on Earth and our active years are further limited, we would want to spend that time wisely on things that matter to us. The possibility of end should help us travel better on our journey of life, meet the right people, go to the right places, participate in the appropriate activities, and spend our time better.

If you feel you are already too busy to think about anything else, do not watch TV or any other video content for one weekend, and do not engage in social media. You will realise that time we have plenty of, it's our will that these websites, TV, and streaming platforms have taken control of. Unfortunately, we are so enamoured by the make-believe world that we forget to see around and inside.

So I am in my mid-thirties; I realise that time is running away, and I do not want to have regrets later. Not having regrets later in my life has been one of my most potent driving forces. So now, whatever I do, I end up asking myself this question:

Is it relevant to me right now, and will it be relevant to me after ten years?

That has helped me cut down on a lot of time-wasting. Right now, I spend very little time on social media. Most of what I do is for my professional upliftment. I make sure that whatever I post is relevant to others, so I do not end up wasting the time of others.

Along with our time, we need to respect the time of others as well. Once we are aware of the importance of our time, we are unlikely to waste the time of others. We are unlikely to spend it on frivolous activities, such as gossiping.

I have all but stopped watching TV or content. Even when I watch, I avoid watching shows and prefer movies since sitcoms demand too much time, which I am now not willing to spend. I watch movies with my family sometimes. We try to make it an event with popcorn and a cosy setting. Such family time gives me both comfort and entertainment. That is time well spent.

Not long ago, I was becoming a two-trick pony, office in the day, TV in the evening. I wasted my time in unimaginable ways. It was not only making my mind dull; I was also losing out on my health. It is well known that you feel hungrier when you are passively watching TV. So, I ate junk, lots of it, while watching TV and that too late into the night. Time went by quickly before I realised what I had done to my health. I weighed 97 kg and felt embarrassed.

I wanted to watch all shows and movies. I tried to quickly watch all episodes of the shows. I was binge-watching and binge-eating and cutting down on my sleep time. Over this, there was FOMO for news, information, and content. When you get stuck in this cycle, it becomes difficult to break out of it. Conscious effort is needed; small steps make a big difference.

I started out by going for a thirty-minute jog in the park three times a week. The beauty of our mind is that it adapts, and if you persist, it adapts quickly. Since I started exercising, I felt tired in the evening, so late-night TV watching was cut down. Eventually, I made several changes to my lifestyle to bring my health and time under my control.

So, if you want to save your time, look for ways and options to do that. Maybe you can learn a skill that can save you time, such as touch typing, start using software or a tool that can help you save time, and maybe delegate non-essential tasks. Invest in such skills or tools since nothing can be more wasteful than wasted time.

Some of these aspects have been discussed in other parts of this book, and I am not repeating them here to save your valuable time.

Conclusion

Time is the most precious commodity we have. It's the one resource that we can never get back, the one constant that weaves through every aspect of our lives. How we choose to spend our time, moment by moment, day by day, ultimately shapes the contours of our existence.

When we learn to master our relationship with time, we tap into a profound source of clarity, productivity and fulfilment.

One of the key insights about time is that it is not a linear, fixed entity, but rather a fluid and subjective experience. The way we perceive and utilise time is deeply influenced by our mental and emotional states, our values and priorities, and the quality of our presence and engagement. By becoming more conscious of these factors, we can learn to bend time to our will and make the most of every moment.

Another crucial aspect of mastering time is learning to balance the competing demands of urgency and importance. In the rush of daily life, it's easy to get caught up in the urgent tasks that demand our immediate attention, at the expense of the important work that moves us closer to our long-term goals and deepest values. By regularly stepping back to reassess our priorities and allocating our time accordingly, we can ensure that we're investing in what truly matters.

Effective time management also requires a blend of discipline and flexibility. On one hand, creating and sticking to a structured schedule can help us stay focused, avoid distractions, and make steady progress on our goals. On the other hand, being too rigid can lead to burnout and a lack of adaptability when unexpected challenges or opportunities arise. The key is to find a rhythm that works for us and to build in buffers and margins for rest, reflection, and spontaneity.

Ultimately, the way we relate to time reflects the way we relate to life itself. When we approach time with a sense of scarcity, rushing from one thing to the next and lamenting how little of it we have, we breed stress, resentment, and a feeling of never enough. But when we approach time with a sense of abundance, savouring each moment and trusting in the natural unfolding of things, we cultivate a deeper sense of peace, presence, and gratitude.

The beauty of mastering our relationship with time is that it has a ripple effect on every area of our lives. As we become more intentional and effective in our use of time, we naturally become more focused, productive, and fulfilled in our work. We have more energy and presence to invest in our relationships and personal growth. We create more space for the activities and experiences that truly light us up.

The next time you find yourself feeling rushed, overwhelmed, or as if there's never enough time, remember that you have a choice. You can let time control you, or you can learn to master it. You can approach each moment as a precious gift, an opportunity to align your actions with your deepest values and aspirations.

Time is not just a measure of minutes and hours, but a measure of life itself. It's the canvas upon which we paint the masterpiece of our existence, stroke by stroke, choice by choice. By learning to master our relationship with time, we reclaim our power to create a life of purpose, meaning, and true prosperity. We remember that every moment is a chance to begin again, to choose differently, to step into the fullness of our potential. And that is the greatest gift of all.

Digital Detoxification

Silence is the language of God, all else is poor translation.

– Rumi (13th-century Persian poet)

We are part of the generation that has seen the transition from the analogue to the digital. We have seen the invention, development, and proliferation of the internet. We are the Millennials. We are living through history in the making. There has never been any other generation that would have gone through a transition and transformation of this stature, primarily brought about by the internet.

The problem of living through this ginormous transition is that we do not know how much digitisation is enough. Moreover, since we are in the transition process, whether we like it or not, we are the guinea pigs of this transformational experiment. Furthermore, we are experiencing the teething troubles of this transition, such as the digital divide, privacy concerns, online frauds, etc.

Where does it stop? Well, it doesn't. But we can. How many smartphones, laptops, tablets, smartwatches, smart speakers, and smart home devices do we need?

At one point in time, I was juggling between so many apparently intelligent devices that I literally became incapable of concentrating on any one thing. It has now been scientifically proven that our attention span has reduced to a level never seen before.

I was so engrossed in looking at the notifications on these devices that I found myself struggling to do one thing at a time. It was as if I was forced to become a multitasker, which is a different monster altogether. Moreover, I developed this OCD of keeping my devices and gadgets charged most of the time, lest I miss out on any critical text or email. As a result, my dependency on these gadgets increased. These devices, which are supposed to make life easier, were doing precisely the opposite.

I decided to take action before it was too late. I decided to curb my shiny objects syndrome and stop buying new devices unless they served a specific purpose. I also decided to retire one device every time a new device is to be purchased. I stopped using my smartwatch since I did not find it serving an essential purpose and went back to my old watch collection, which does not need charging every day. I realised that just one less device to charge can be a pleasant experience in itself. I took other small steps to reduce my dependency and increase productivity. This entire book is written on paper and will be typed or dictated onto the laptop for editing. This hand-mind coordination does not apply when we are typing. Typing does not engage the right brain the way writing does, and I feel less creative while typing than writing on paper. Maybe that will change when the transition to digital is complete, but this is how we are wired for now.

I have stopped tracking every aspect of my life; I do not want to know how many steps I have taken today, how many floors I have climbed today, how many days of exercise I have had, or how many hours of meditation I have completed.

I do not keep my phone on my bedside table; I avoid watching any screen after 9 PM. These are some steps that are helping me cope with a digital transition. I also suggest some other steps for digital detoxification:

- Fix a time, or two times a day, for checking and responding to your emails
- Delete apps you do not use or have not used in the last 30 days.
- Turn off notifications for all non-essential apps.
- Leave your phone outside your bedroom when you're going off to sleep.
- Do not look at screens at least 30 minutes before you plan to go to sleep.
- Do not look at screens at least for one hour after you wake up.
- Stop yourself from looking at your phone every few minutes.

- Read the good old newspaper instead of reading news on a tab or laptop or on your Twitter feed. The worldwide web has been built to keep you engaged. Before you know it, instead of reading the news, you will be watching cat videos on YouTube.
- Use tools like 'Screen time' and 'Digital well-being' on your mobile devices. Believe it or not, YouTube has a setting that lets you know when it is time for you to go to sleep. As ironical as it may seem, use these digital tools for reminding yourself to get off your digital devices.
- Find new hobbies and activities which do not need you to use devices. These could be things like playing sudoku in the newspaper or playing boardgames or card games like 'Go fish' with family.
- Opt for paper books over e-books when you can.

The more connected we are with the world, the more disconnected we are getting with ourselves. If connecting all the computers and smartphones with each other through the internet was not enough, technology has now moved on to conquer another bastion. The Internet of Things or IoT is now being used to connect our lightbulbs, televisions, air conditioners, microwaves, refrigerators, etc., with the internet, calling them smart devices. These smart devices are actually dumbing us down. We do not really need a fridge to remind us what we need to get from the market, and we do not need our lightbulbs to turn on and off at a scheduled time. # and @ have become as valuable as ₹ and $, if not more.

All said and done, digitalisation and devices are here to stay and proliferate. We need to arm ourselves to not get disoriented and use these devices for the purpose they have been built, that is, to simplify our lives and not complicate them.

Conclusion

In our modern, hyper-connected world, digital technology has become an integral part of our daily lives. From the moment we wake up to the moment we go to sleep, we are constantly bombarded with emails, notifications, social media updates, and a never-ending stream of digital content. While these tools have undoubtedly brought many benefits and conveniences, they have also created a new set of challenges for our mental health, relationships, and overall well-being. This is where the practice of digital detoxification comes in.

Digital detoxification is the conscious choice to unplug from digital devices and platforms for a set period of time in order to reconnect with ourselves, others, and the world around us. It's a way of reclaiming our time, attention, and energy from the constant pull of the digital realm and rediscovering the simple joys and richness of life beyond the screen.

One of the key benefits of digital detoxification is the opportunity to reduce stress and anxiety. By stepping away from the constant barrage of information and stimulation, we give our minds a chance to rest, recharge, and process our experiences. We create space for stillness, reflection, and a deeper connection to our inner world. We remember what it feels like to be fully present and engaged in the moment, without the constant distraction and comparison that digital media often breeds.

Digital detoxification also allows us to cultivate more meaningful relationships and experiences. When we're not constantly tethered to our devices, we're more likely to have face-to-face conversations, engage in shared activities, and create memories that last. We're more attuned to the needs and feelings of others and more able to give them our full attention and presence. We remember the value of human connection and the depth of experience that can only be found in the real-world.

Another important aspect of digital detoxification is the opportunity to reconnect with our own creativity, curiosity, and sense of purpose. When we're not constantly consuming digital content, we create space for our own ideas and inspirations to emerge. We rediscover the joy of learning, exploring, and creating for its own sake, rather than for the validation of likes and shares. We tap into a deeper sense of meaning and fulfilment that comes from aligning our actions with our values and passions.

Of course, digital detoxification doesn't mean completely abandoning technology forever. It's about finding a healthy balance that works for us and being intentional about how we use digital tools to support our well-being and goals. It's about setting clear boundaries around our digital consumption and regularly unplugging to give ourselves the gift of presence and perspective.

The beauty of digital detoxification is that it's a practice that anyone can start at any time. Whether it's committing to a daily device-free hour, a weekly digital sabbath, or a longer retreat from technology, every small step counts. The key is to approach it with curiosity, self-compassion, and a willingness to experiment and adjust as we go.

The next time you find yourself feeling overwhelmed, scattered, or disconnected, consider the power of digital detoxification. Give yourself permission to unplug, breathe, and reconnect with what truly matters. Trust that by creating space for stillness and presence, you are nourishing your mind, body, and soul in ways that no amount of digital stimulation can replace.

Digital detoxification is about reclaiming our humanity in an increasingly digitised world. It's about remembering that we are more than our online personas, more than the sum of our likes and followers. We are living, breathing beings with a deep need for connection, meaning, and authentic experience. By learning to use technology mindfully and intentionally, and regularly unplugging to savour the richness of life beyond the screen, we open ourselves up to a world of greater joy, creativity, and true fulfilment. And that is the greatest gift we can give ourselves in the digital age.

Social Media

Distracted from distraction by distraction.

– T.S. Eliot

When social networking first arrived, who would have thought that it would become the new normal? Who would have thought that people would find it suitable, and even preferable, to announce their life events, feelings, and achievements online to a group of people who may or may not be interested in hearing about them?

Human beings are driven by ego; we are more interested in our own lives. In most cases, our interest in someone else's life is restricted to knowing about it only to compare it with ours. Is the other person enjoying, achieving, or earning more than I? For the person posting something on social media, the idea is to attract attention, while for the person looking at the post, the intention is to compare with themselves. Neither is better than the other.

Social media encourages egoistic showcasing. The emotions it leads to are envy and jealousy. Of course, like with everything else in the world, there are exceptions.

Many use social media to spread awareness about socially relevant issues, encourage charity, promote personal growth, promote businesses, etc. Unfortunately, these ideas are not attractive to most people. They do not create the sensationalism that a controversial tweet of a celebrity would make. Constructive use of social media is far too less compared to its undesirable consequences. Long-term effects are still being studied, but some studies have shown a link between social media and aggravation of mental health issues.

Most people are just browsing through social media as if they are browsing through other people's real lives, and nothing could be farther from the truth. When we post something for the world to see, we are putting our best foot forward. It is as if we are living a scripted life through social media. We satisfy our ego and inner desires to feel important and loved when we fish for those likes, views, and retweets.

A few years back, while going through my social media feed, I started questioning my life, choices, and achievements. I was so perturbed by my feelings and emotions that poured out that I decided to quit social media. I completely stopped using social media for around four years. I reactivated my social media handles during the lockdown imposed after the Covid-19 pandemic made its presence felt, and everything moved online. It was a time when we needed social media to keep up with people we know and care for and stay in the know about happenings around us. It was the time when social media supplemented the news which was presented by the media houses. So what happened when I quit social media? Did someone miss me, and what happened when I joined back? Did someone celebrate that? Of course, neither of those things happened or were expected to happen. On a digital platform, none of us matter. Our actual social circle is built up of a few close aides who are with you and have been with you through thick and thin.

My learnings from social media have been that use it for whatever purpose you want; however, do not rely on it to provide you with the actual picture of your true social standing. You may not be anything to everyone, but you are something to someone, and that's what matters.

Know the purpose of using social media; it could be for keeping in touch with your friends and family, for entertainment, for marketing or any other purpose. It is incredible to see how many people consider social media and even multi-player video games equivalent to socialising, especially during the pandemic period. According to Newzoo's Global Games Market Report for 2020, socialising was the second most cited reason for playing more games. So be aware of the purpose of using social media, and you will save yourself from disillusionment, intimidation and dejection, which troubles many among us these days.

I do not browse social media. I sometimes post if I have something interesting to say and respond to any comments on the posts. I use it only for this specific purpose, and that helps me maintain my sanity. Social media can make you feel that the world is moving so fast when it is not. The world is still the same; technology has just let us inside the lives of others, at least the good part of their lives. When we see so many people doing so many exciting things, travelling, creating, achieving, we are bound to feel overwhelmed. We are not living their lives, we are living ours, and we start questioning our lives, travels, creations, achievements. We start seeing the futility of our lives. We begin to think that we put in so much hard work, yet we achieve nothing or create nothing or the fact that we do not travel where everyone in the world seems to be travelling.

We have been given a gateway into a diamond museum. We do not know how and from where those diamonds were collected, how much effort went into it. Next time you browse through your social media feed, imagine it to be a museum of everyone's good life. The other part of life, the failures, the hard work, the loss and suffering, the regular and the mundane, are the parts that are left out of social media posts, just like the curator leaves ordinary artefacts from the display of the museum.

Conclusion

Social media has revolutionised the way we connect, communicate, and consume information in the digital age. Platforms like Facebook, Twitter, Instagram, and LinkedIn have become ubiquitous in our daily lives, offering unprecedented opportunities for networking, self-expression, and access to a global community. However, as with any powerful tool, social media also presents a range of challenges and pitfalls that require mindful navigation to ensure our well-being and success in the online world.

One of the key benefits of social media is its ability to foster connections and communities across geographical and cultural boundaries. Through these platforms, we can find and engage with like-minded individuals, build relationships with mentors and collaborators, and expand our personal and professional networks in ways that were once impossible. Social media has democratised access to information and influence, giving voice to diverse perspectives and enabling grassroots movements for social change.

At the same time, the constant connectivity and instant gratification of social media can also breed a range of negative effects. The pressure to curate a perfect online persona can lead to feelings of inadequacy, self-doubt, and a distorted sense of reality. The endless scroll of carefully curated highlight reels can fuel comparison, envy, and a sense of missing out. The anonymity and distance of online interactions can enable bullying, harassment, and the spread of misinformation and hate speech.

To navigate the complex landscape of social media in a healthy and productive way, it's essential to approach these platforms with intentionality, self-awareness, and clear boundaries. This means being selective about the accounts we follow, the content we consume, and the interactions we engage in. It means regularly unplugging and creating space for real-world experiences and relationships. It means using social media as a tool for authentic self-expression, meaningful connection, and positive impact rather than a measure of self-worth or a substitute for real-life.

Another key aspect of mindful social media use is developing a critical lens for the information and influences we encounter online. In an era of fake news, echo chambers, and algorithmic bias, it's crucial to fact-check sources, seek out diverse perspectives, and engage in respectful dialogue across differences. By approaching social media with a growth mindset, we can use these platforms as a tool for learning, personal development, and collaborative problem-solving.

Ultimately, the impact of social media on our lives depends on how we choose to use it. When approached with intention, self-awareness, and a commitment to authentic connection and positive impact, these platforms can be a powerful tool for personal and collective growth. But when used mindlessly, compulsively, or as a substitute for real-world engagement, they can also breed disconnection, division, and distress.

The beauty of mindful social media use is that it allows us to harness the best of what these platforms have to offer while minimising their potential downsides. By setting clear intentions and boundaries, cultivating a healthy online environment, and regularly unplugging to nurture our real-world relationships and experiences, we can use social media to support our well-being and success.

The next time you find yourself scrolling through your social media feeds, take a moment to check in with yourself. Ask yourself what you're really looking for in that moment and whether social media is the best way to meet that need. Remember that your worth and happiness come from within, not from the fleeting validation of likes and shares.

Social media is just a tool – it's up to us to use it wisely and purposefully. By approaching these platforms with mindfulness, authenticity, and a commitment to positive impact, we can create an online world that reflects the best of our shared humanity. We can use social media not just to connect, but to truly see and support one another in our journey of growth and becoming. And that is the greatest promise of the digital age.

Finances

Live below your means. Save for the future. Reduce your risk.

– Benjamin Franklin (1706–1790)

In our 20s, we get a taste of money and the independence it brings. We enjoy the freedom of spending money. We feel a sense of achievement when we buy our first car or our first house.

But it is not always so straightforward with money. Most of us have a love-hate relationship with money. We may have enough, but we always want more. There is no problem in wanting more. Wanting something can be the motivating factor for achieving something. However, to receive something that we want, we will also have to give something in exchange. If you want more money, you will need to spend more time and energy earning that money. If you can't do that, do not blame the world.

I must have been 35 or 36 when, one fine day, while doing some banking transaction, it dawned on me that I had no idea where I had spent all the money I had earned in the last 10 to 12 years of work. I could think of some considerable expenses and spending, but where did the rest of the money go? It got me thinking, and I concluded that I was not in control of my finances, which got me into action immediately.

In our 30s, we realise the importance of money. It is a blessing and a curse. It is never adequate. We always have less, and we always want more of it. The trouble was that I was not concerned with having less or more of it. I was more concerned with having control over it, which disturbed me.

I spent a few days trying to figure out what was happening, and I realised that a more important question was, why was it happening? It became clear to me that I was letting this vital part of my life slip by. Money does not manage itself unattended, and there is more to it than just earning it and spending it. I immediately knew I needed a course correction, and what better way to start than to learn about it. Doing something without knowledge is like shooting in the dark; you may hit or miss the target. But if you gain knowledge about something, then you will not be directionless. It is only with the knowledge that you will know where to start. Once you know the source of information, you can always go back for guidance and more information.

I started reading up on personal finance and money management. There are several books and websites with authentic information.

At one point in time, I was overwhelmed with too much information and started thinking of contacting a financial adviser. I, however, decided to give it another shot and cut back on the information I was devouring. Information overload can make you fall back, and we need to draw a line somewhere.

I restricted myself to some fundamental but genuine sources of information. Eventually, I realised it was no rocket science. All I needed was a plan of investment and monitoring of my assets at regular intervals. Like everything else in life, if my investments were going off course, I would realign my investments. I learnt about the concepts of equity and debt and the allocation of funds to these two investment options.

I had burnt my fingers in the stock market earlier. However, I started looking at it again, this time with a different perspective. That's what happens, right? When you have the correct information and knowledge, the same thing you had been looking at for a long time starts appearing different. For example, suppose a child was misbehaving. In that case, your first instinct might be to scold her. However, what if you were informed that she had not slept properly and was irritable because of a lack of sleep? You may look at the situation differently. You may change your plan from scolding to helping the child sleep.

I thought of the equity markets as a gambling place, and frankly, I still see it as prone to manipulation.

However, this time I was entering the lion's den, knowing that I just might see a lion. I had spent some time learning the ropes and wanted to try out my knowledge. I learnt to understand the fundamentals and the technical charts as well. I realised how foolish it was of me to invest in equities without that knowledge.

For equity investments, you need three things: money, knowledge, and patience. However, I also realised that it is not easy to keep up with the stock market. For that reason, investments in mutual funds, both equity and debt, were also good options. This is especially useful when we have to manage our investments along with our work responsibilities.

It is not possible to lay down all the information here. However, I would still like to lay down some basic rules for you to start with. If you are already managing your investments, consider these as just reminders. Remember that I am not a financial adviser. The information I am putting down here is what I have learnt from experience and from experts in the field. Depending on your needs and circumstances, it may be better to have the experts manage your money and investments.

Universal Principles

- Do your own research and go on your own investment journey. Do not expect money to manage on its own; it doesn't happen.

- Gain as much knowledge as you can. You will need it even if you plan to hire a financial adviser to manage your finances.
- Set your life goals. Then, decide your financial goals based on your life goals. For example, in three years, I want to buy a new house. I need to factor in the instalments I will be paying. In five years, I will need to buy a new car. In 10 years, my daughter will need to go to college, maybe in a foreign country.
- Keep all information on your investments organised and available for easy reference.
- Do not spend all your money. If required, open a separate account to transfer the amount needed for your expenses, including shopping and entertainment. The remaining money in your primary account, which may be your salary account, can be earmarked for investments.
- Create an emergency fund and add to it regularly. As a thumb rule, your emergency fund should have an amount equal to 3 to 6 months of expenses. Start early to build your emergency fund for unforeseen circumstances.
- Keep yourself updated on the new schemes, concepts and investment options regularly introduced by the government and financial institutions.

Equity and Debt

- If you plan to invest in the stock market, learn about reading the company's fundamentals for long-term investments.
- If you also want to do short-term trading, you will need to master reading the technical charts such as RSI, MACD, Bollinger band, and EMA to not end up buying shares at the wrong time and at the wrong price.
- As a thumb rule, a hundred minus your age should be your equity allocation, and the rest should be in debt instruments. For example, if you are 35, then (100-35=65) 65% of your investment can be in equity and the rest in debt instruments. Rebalance the equity-debt ratio every few years.
- Keep most of your savings in debt instruments such as debt funds or Fixed Deposits instead of your savings account.
- Invest in some good government-backed investment schemes such as PPF and NPS. Prolong your PPF investments by extending the PPF account every five years after the initial 15 years for as long as you can to enjoy the benefits of compounding.
- Mutual funds have lesser risk and, therefore, lesser returns, but they can be effective for a longer time horizon.

- Do not get attached to any particular share, mutual fund, debt fund, etc. They are just investment options. If they are not giving adequate returns, liquidate and move on to another option.

Real Estate

- Some may not agree with me, but it is better to buy a house for yourself than to stay in rented accommodation. Some people argue that it is better to invest that money and earn more returns than the appreciation you would enjoy from your own property. I disagree. It is not just the appreciation or the return that you can make. It is also the psychological feeling of contentment and satisfaction when living in a home you own. The money you pay to a landlord is gone forever. In contrast, the money you invest in your own property stays with you and appreciates over time. So whenever you are comfortable with taking that leap, invest in a home.

- When buying a house, keep these three rules in mind: Location, Location and Location.

- If you plan to buy another property after you have invested in a home, consider commercial properties rather than residential ones. Commercial properties offer better returns on investment.

Insurance

- Unless you have an additional residential property at your disposal, buy term insurance.
- Do not buy insurance for the purpose of investments. Keep your investment and your insurance products separate.
- Invest in health insurance, it is getting more and more essential. You can also consider buying critical illness insurance for better risk cover.
- An insurance product called 'Super Top-Up' insurance expands your insurance coverage over and above your existing insurance or the amount you are willing to bear on your own. Explore this product to see if it suits your needs.

Remember, these are only a few things I feel are essential. First, you must do your own research and walk on your investment journey on your own. Also, remember, if something appears too good to be true, it probably is.

Do not be too attached to money. There will be times when you will have less of it and times when you will have more of it. If you are going through a rough patch financially, do not stop taking action. Doing nothing will not help; crying over it will not help. Be aware that times, both good and bad, come and go. You have to work through them with equanimity. If you are going through a good phase, enjoy your time fully. Be satisfied but do not let it get to your head.

If the universe has bestowed you with wealth, appreciate it, be grateful for it. But don't let ego drive you from thereon. As a lawyer, I have dealt with many businesses and businessmen, big and small. I have seen the biggest of companies go down in no time. I have seen people running away and hiding from creditors. But, I have also seen people managing their work through the worst of times by being innovative, action-oriented, and, more than anything, being positive.

Conclusion

Finances play a crucial role in our lives, influencing our daily decisions, long-term goals, and overall sense of security and well-being. How we earn, save, invest, and spend our money not only reflects our practical needs and desires but also our values, priorities, and relationship with abundance and scarcity. By developing a mindful and proactive approach to financial management, we can create a foundation of stability and freedom that supports our personal growth and life purpose.

One of the key aspects of financial wellness is creating a clear and realistic budget. This means taking an honest look at our income and expenses, distinguishing between needs and wants, and aligning our spending with our values and goals. By tracking our cash flow and making informed choices about where to allocate our resources, we can avoid the stress and limitations of living paycheck to paycheck and start building a buffer of savings and investments.

Another crucial component of financial health is understanding and managing debt. While some forms of debt, such as mortgages or business loans, can be strategic tools for building wealth, high-interest consumer debt can quickly spiral into a cycle of stress and limitation. By proactively addressing debt through strategies like consolidation, negotiation, and accelerated repayment, we can free up more of our income for saving, investing, and enjoying life.

Beyond budgeting and debt management, cultivating a long-term perspective on wealth is essential for financial success. This means setting clear financial goals, creating a plan to reach them, and consistently following through with discipline and adaptability. Whether it's saving for a down payment, starting a business, or securing a comfortable retirement, having a vision and strategy for our financial future gives us a sense of purpose and motivation in our daily money choices.

Ultimately, a healthy relationship with money is about more than just numbers in a bank account. It's about aligning our financial habits with our deepest values and aspirations. It's about using money as a tool for creating experiences, relationships, and contributions that enrich our lives and the lives of others. It's about cultivating an attitude of abundance, gratitude, and generosity, recognising that true wealth is not just about what we have, but who we become in the process.

The beauty of mindful financial management is that it's a skill that anyone can learn and practice, regardless of their current income or circumstances. By educating ourselves about personal finance, seeking guidance from mentors and professionals, and consistently applying best practices in our daily lives, we can transform our relationship with money from one of stress and scarcity to one of empowerment and abundance.

The next time you find yourself making a financial decision, take a moment to reflect on your values, goals, and long-term vision. Ask yourself if this choice aligns with your deepest priorities and aspirations, and if it moves you closer to the life you truly want to live.

Remember that your financial journey is unique, and there will be ups and downs along the way. But by approaching money with mindfulness, integrity, and a commitment to growth and service, you can create a legacy of abundance and impact that extends far beyond your bank account.

Financial wellness is about more than just security and freedom – it's about living a life of purpose, joy, and contribution. It's about using the resources we've been given to create a world of greater opportunity, connection, and prosperity for all. By mastering the art of money management and aligning our finances with our highest values, we open ourselves up to a lifetime of abundance, resilience, and meaningful success. And that is the greatest wealth we can create.

Finding Balance

Samatvam yoga uchchyate.

– Bhagavad Gita (Chapter 2, Verse 48)

Equanimity is called yoga.

There are so many aspects of life that require us to maintain balance. We need to balance our work and life, balance our diet to get all the required nutrition, and balance our budget between our needs and wants. If your balance is tilted towards one side, the other side will suffer. For example, if you are inclined more towards work, your life will suffer, and vice versa.

I had been told that achievement is making a name for yourself. This name could come through fame, power, or money. With time, I have realised that that was flawed teaching. I believe that achievement means different things to different people. My idea of achievement is a simple life, which does not mean leading an ordinary life. We can have an extraordinary yet simple life. My idea of a simple life is one in which all aspects of life that I consider essential have been equally covered, which include my health, family, and profession, in that order. My achievement would be a life that balances all these aspects. If the balance tilts more towards one, the other two will suffer. For example, if it leans more towards the profession, family and health will suffer.

To maintain these external balances, the prerequisite is to keep our inner balance. I believe that to have balance in our life, we need to balance our minds. A balanced state of mind will help you achieve all other balances relatively quickly.

Maintaining a balanced state of mind is a superpower and comes with extreme perseverance. I am not suggesting that you will not feel the emotions you are supposed to when you have a balanced mind. You feel the same feelings of joy, love, anger, sadness, and fear. Still, you go through those emotions knowing that the circumstances that lead to those emotions in me are temporary. Therefore, my feelings, which are a direct consequence of those circumstances, are also impermanent.

So, if I have had a desire to buy a house or a desire to get a job in a particular company, and that desire gets fulfilled, I feel the joy and happiness that comes from fulfilling a wish, but that is something momentary. So, my next feeling is of satisfaction that my actions are leading to positive consequences. Then, my next thought is to get back to doing further work, further action, to keep experiencing the positive results of that work.

Now, if I am faced with negative emotions, such as anger and rage, for example, while driving on Delhi roads, I am again aware that the situation is momentary and my anger is transient. I will soon reach my destination, and I only need to focus on driving when I am on the road.

The above two situations are easier to manage with the knowledge and awareness of our thoughts and emotions. Symbolism can also help. For example, a symbol in your car can help you remember that anger while driving is futile, and it does nothing except hurt you mentally and emotionally. Furthermore, it is comparatively easier to train your mind to deal with such situations since you know there is no end to desires (and there is no end to driving).

How about situations which are more long-lasting, such as being stuck in a job you don't like, or with a boss you don't approve of, or with a colleague who does not have anything positive to say about anyone? What about the situation where you experience an unspeakable loss, such as the death of a loved one? How could you possibly maintain a balanced state of mind in such overwhelming situations?

The first thing you need to do is accept that most external factors are not in your control. As I have mentioned elsewhere, acceptance is the most promising tool to bring about a profound change in yourself. You cannot change your family, but you can accept them. You cannot change your circumstances, but you can accept them. Once you accept the people in your life and the circumstances you face, you can change yourself to deal with those circumstances. You can mould yourself.

The second thing you need to understand is that how you react to such an external factor is under your control. Your reaction to an external situation is a choice you make at that moment. You could respond differently on two different occasions when faced with a similar situation. For example, you go to a restaurant and are offered a buffet or an a-la-carte menu. You go for the buffet to enjoy more options. Next time you go to the same restaurant and are offered the same choices, you start thinking that you overate last time only because you opted for the buffet. So, you opt for the a-la-carte menu this time. Your past experience allowed you to assess and analyse. Even though you were faced with a similar situation, you made a different choice to better suit your needs.

Third, and most importantly, you can train your mind. The mind is malleable. It can be trained to reduce reaction time, react differently, look at a situation differently, and analyse and respond.

As you may have gathered, such training of the mind is achieved through meditation. That is the best way to control your actions and reactions and train your mind to act or react in a particular way.

Several external factors also help you achieve and maintain that balanced state of mind, one of which is simplicity. A simple life and simple living act as a shield against negativity. It gives you strength of mind and character. On the other hand, a complicated life, complex relationships, and manipulating others are all sources of negative emotions. In the same manner, it is natural to feel happy and proud of achieving something or fulfilling any desire; however, if that pride increases uncontrolled, it turns into ego, which dissuades spiritual well-being. So, both positive and negative emotions will prevent you from having a balanced state of mind and take you off the path of equanimity and spirituality.

To prevent this, you will need to control both internal and external stimuli. Internal provocations can be controlled through meditation, and external motivations are regulated through simple living.

What about situations of extreme loss or other conditions which are not under anyone's control? The fact of the matter is that you will face such problems, whether you like it or not. These situations can make you forget all your training. Nothing has prepared you for dealing with such situations. They are overwhelming and give you a feeling of helplessness. In times like these, it may seem almost impossible, but one thing can be done to get a grip on yourself.

I went through such a situation when I lost my sister. Unfortunately, I was only 14, and I did not have the tools to deal with the situation. I now understand that it is almost impossible to train your mind for such life events. Still, its impact can be reduced if we engage ourselves in something constructive. That will help you take your mind off the event and calm you. Once you are calm, then other steps can be taken to get your mind back on track. These constructive activities could be pursuing a hobby, learning a new skill, volunteering at some charity event, writing a book, etc. It does not have to be a commercial endeavour; anything under the sun that can keep you productively engaged is advisable.

Most external factors are not in our control. If we can detach ourselves from a situation, person, or thing leading to negative emotions, we should. If we can't separate, then we should look to turn the situation positive. Suppose the problem is such that it cannot be manipulated. In that case, we should start doing something constructive at the earliest possible opportunity, which can help us maintain the positive outlook that we strive for.

There is a higher level of balance that needs to be maintained: the balance of nature. If we do not balance nature with industrialisation, then life on Earth, including the life of human beings, will suffer. That is why sustainable development is something that the human race should strive for. It should do everything to progress without damaging the environment.

This balance can happen if we stop thinking of ourselves as the most superior beings in nature. The human race needs to think spiritually, and that process starts with each one of us. We need to think of ourselves as connected with each other at a spiritual level. When we are making a decision, we need to ensure the safety and sustainability of our spiritual companions. This will help bring more harmony and balance in nature and in our lives.

The concept of one consciousness of which we all are a part, as advocated by Neem Karoli Baba and later by his disciple, Baba Ram Dass, brings harmonious living into fruition. When you see everything and every person as a spiritual being, you see the beauty in everything that surrounds you. You feel more grateful and connected to the world and to every being in the world. This brings about spiritual progress, peace, and balance in your life.

Conclusion

In the fast-paced, ever-changing landscape of modern life, finding balance can feel like an elusive goal. We are constantly juggling the demands of work, family, relationships, personal growth, and self-care, often feeling like we're running on a treadmill that never stops. But while perfect balance may be a myth, cultivating a sense of harmony, purpose, and joy amidst the chaos is not only possible but essential for our well-being and success.

At its core, finding balance is about aligning our time, energy, and attention with our deepest values and priorities. It's about getting clear on what truly matters to us and making conscious choices to invest in those areas, even when it means saying no to other demands and distractions. It's about creating a life that feels authentic, meaningful, and sustainable rather than one that leaves us feeling depleted, disconnected, and unfulfiled.

One of the key aspects of finding balance is learning to set healthy boundaries. This means knowing our limits, communicating our needs, and being willing to say no to requests or invitations that don't align with our priorities. It means carving out non-negotiable time for rest, self-care, and the activities that recharge and inspire us. It means letting go of the guilt and perfectionism that often drive us to overextend ourselves and trusting that by taking care of ourselves first, we can show up more fully and effectively in all areas of life.

Another crucial component of balance is cultivating mindfulness and presence. In a world of constant stimulation and distraction, it's easy to get caught up in the noise and lose touch with the moment-to-moment experience of our lives. By practising mindfulness through techniques like meditation, deep breathing, and sensory awareness, we can train our minds to be more focused, grounded, and attuned to the richness of the present. We can learn to savour the simple joys and beauty that surround us, rather than always chasing the next goal or achievement.

Ultimately, finding balance is a dynamic and ongoing process, not a fixed destination. As our lives and circumstances change, so too must our strategies for maintaining harmony and well-being. This requires a willingness to be flexible, adaptable, and compassionate with ourselves, recognising that what works in one season of life may not work in another. It means being open to experimentation, learning, and growth, and trusting that by staying true to our core values and needs, we can navigate the ups and downs of life with greater resilience and grace.

The beauty of finding balance is that it allows us to show up as our best selves in all areas of life. When we're not constantly running on empty, we have more energy, creativity, and presence to bring to our work, relationships, and personal pursuits. We're more able to handle challenges and setbacks with perspective and poise, knowing that our self-worth and happiness don't hinge on external outcomes. We're more able to connect deeply and authentically with others, creating a sense of community and support that sustains us through life's journey.

The next time you find yourself feeling overwhelmed, scattered, or out of sync, remember that balance is not about perfection, but about intention. It's about making small, consistent choices that align with your values and nourish your mind, body, and soul. It's about learning to listen to your own inner wisdom and honouring your unique needs and rhythms.

Finding balance is about creating a life that feels like a true reflection of who you are and what you stand for. It's about embracing the messiness and imperfection of the human experience while still striving for growth, meaning, and contribution. By cultivating a sense of inner harmony and purpose, you become a force for positive change in your own life and the lives of those around you. And that is the greatest balance of all.

Decision Making

Viveka eva karmasaadhanam.

– Hitopadesha (3rd century BCE)

Discernment is the means to action.

We are a generation spoilt for choice. We consider having a choice a right. We live in a constant state of choice overload. From books to read to professions to pursue, we have too many options and too little time. Making a choice has become a tough job. On top of that, there is a fear that I might make the wrong decision. There is also the fear of missing out; what if I decide and some other option was a better fit for me? Some other worries may also plague our decision-making; I may fear that others will not like my decision. All these fears may either prevent us altogether from making a decision or from making the correct decision.

A question arises: what is a correct decision? Well, there isn't any, and at the same time, all of them are. There are no good or bad decisions, just the ones you need to take now. You may have observed that, at least sometimes, how you frame your thoughts can help you get over the consequences of a decision you have taken.

For example, suppose you own some shares which were in losses for the longest time. One day you see that they are now in profit. You fear that they may dip again. Based on your instinct, you decide to sell your shares and make a small profit. After a few days, you observe that the same stock has skyrocketed based on some news. One option is for you to feel unlucky about that and curse your decision, or you can reframe your thoughts to feel satisfied that you showed patience and did not sell them at a loss. Such reframing of thoughts helps us stay more content and happy, but it comes with practice and patience.

There are two aspects of decision-making that I would touch upon. One is the practical aspect, which is a basic set of dos and don'ts you can start applying from day one. This is where quick strategies can be used to make it easier for you to make a decision. The other is the natural aspect of it. When I say natural, what I mean is that decision-making should come naturally to you.

Practical Decision Making

Practical decision-making requires you to take note of the following:

Too many choices are no choices at all. When we are presented with too many choices, we get too overwhelmed to actually make a decision. We would want to avoid such a decision and move on to decisions with fewer options that our brain can quickly process.

The best practical way to decide is to cut down on your options and make a short list. Fewer choices make for better decisions.

Make that choice, take that decision, and after that, do not think if you have made the right choice or not.

There are no good or bad decisions. It is how we frame our minds that decides if we have made the right or wrong choice. So do not dwell on your decision. Decide and move on.

Natural Decision Making

Natural decision-making happens when you are in a position to enjoy the process of decision-making. It is not something that you would avoid. We always have choices available to us. We have to choose every day; we have to make those decisions. If we do not, somebody else will make those decisions for us, in which case, we will be living our life by default and not by design.

All the skills I have mentioned below for natural decision-making are not instant action skills. If you need to make a decision today, you cannot simply apply them. These are life skills and take consistent and persistent effort on your part. Anything meaningful takes time and requires effort. Small steps every day will help you reach a stage when good decisions and good decision-making will come naturally to you. When something comes naturally, it is effortless. When something comes naturally and effortlessly, then you tend to enjoy it rather than dread it.

More than anything else, a certain calmness of the mind is required for sound decision-making. This is because most of our decisions are taken emotionally. Whether we are elated, agitated, or depressed, our emotions define the kind of decisions we take.

Sometimes, we do not even consciously make a decision. Instead, our emotions make those decisions for us. For example, suppose I am deciding on making a significant real estate investment, buying a house for myself and my family. In that case, I could be fearful about the investment I am making. After all, I am investing so much of my hard-earned wealth in one place; or I could be joyful and elated for having received the wealth and opportunity to invest in a house.

Both scenarios are unhealthy for decision-making. I would be blinded by the emotions, which may lead to a decision I may regret later. If I am too fearful, I may just drop the idea or become indecisive or leave it to others to decide for me. If I am too excited, I may just overlook certain vital aspects and invest wrongly. Either way, emotional decisions make for bad investments.

I am deliberately not saying a 'good' or 'correct' decision here. A decision may be right at this time but may turn out to be a wrong decision later. However, I have to make a decision that shows promise to me at this point in time after considering all the practicalities and scenarios. The only way to take a promising decision is by keeping a neutral mindset, a balanced state of mind. Then, I will be able to keep my head clear and think more logically.

Decision-making is the process in which you can use your practice of meditation and self-awareness practically.

- *Meditation* helps you to be in the present moment, to not worry about the past or future. It also enables you to control your thoughts and make your thought pattern malleable, which can be moulded as per your will.
- *Self-awareness* allows you to make decisions with the right attitude. It helps you to make a decision that is in line or in sync with your conscience.
- A balanced state of mind helps you think and act neutrally and logically.

When you decide with these skills by your side, your likelihood of making the right decision increases. Moreover, you will avoid FOMO with such a decision since you will not feel the need to revise your decision and go back to some other option.

These are not skills that you can learn overnight. These are life skills that come with a lot of effort and intention. You need to put a lot of heart into it, but decision-making can be a breeze once you have done it.

Conclusion

Decision-making is a fundamental skill that shapes the course of our lives, both personally and professionally. Every day, we face countless choices, from the seemingly trivial to the truly consequential, that reflect our values, goals, and understanding of ourselves and the world around us. By developing a mindful and strategic approach to decision-making, we can navigate life's challenges and opportunities with greater clarity, confidence, and purpose.

One of the key aspects of effective decision-making is self-awareness. This means taking an honest look at our strengths, weaknesses, biases, and motivations, and understanding how they influence our perceptions and choices. It means getting clear on our core values and long-term goals, and using them as a compass to guide us through the complexity of decision-making. By cultivating a deep understanding of who we are and what we stand for, we can make choices that align with our authentic selves and lead us towards a life of meaning and fulfilment.

Another crucial component of decision-making is information gathering and analysis. In a world of endless data and competing perspectives, it's essential to develop the skills of critical thinking, research, and evaluation.

This means seeking out diverse sources of information, asking probing questions, and considering multiple viewpoints before coming to a conclusion. It means learning to distinguish between facts and opinions, and to recognise the limitations and uncertainties inherent in any decision-making process.

Beyond self-awareness and information analysis, effective decision-making also requires emotional intelligence and intuition. While rational thinking is important, our emotions and gut instincts often hold valuable wisdom and insight that can guide us towards the right path. By learning to tune into our emotional responses and inner voice, we can tap into a deeper level of knowing that goes beyond mere logic and reason. At the same time, it's important to balance intuition with critical thinking and to be aware of how our emotions can sometimes lead us astray.

Ultimately, the art of decision-making is about embracing responsibility and ownership for our choices. While we can't control every outcome or circumstance, we can choose how we respond to them and what we learn from them. By approaching decision-making with a growth mindset and a willingness to adapt and iterate, we can turn even the most challenging choices into opportunities for learning, growth, and transformation.

The beauty of mastering decision-making is that it empowers us to shape our lives and the world around us in meaningful ways. When we make choices that align with our values and vision, we create a ripple effect of positive change that extends far beyond ourselves. We become leaders, innovators, and change-makers, inspiring others with our courage, integrity, and commitment to making a difference.

The next time you face a decision, big or small, take a moment to pause and reflect. Ask yourself what truly matters to you, what information you need to make an informed choice, and what your intuition is telling you. Remember that every decision is an opportunity to learn, grow, and move closer to the life and world you want to create.

Decision-making is not just a skill, but a way of being. It's about living with intention, authenticity, and purpose, and trusting in our ability to navigate the twists and turns of life with wisdom, resilience, and grace. By embracing the art of decision-making, we become the authors of our own stories, the architects of our own futures. And that is the greatest power we can wield.

Relationships and Married Life

To love and be loved is to feel the sun from both sides.

– David Viscott

Marriage is a tough nut to crack. But, for a married person, that one relationship is the crucial factor that defines the remaining aspects of their life. If you are in an unhappy relationship, then everything else, every achievement, seems futile. Everyone goes through their fair share of ups and downs. Of course, it becomes easier if you have a companion to share your life with. But, by no means is it easy. In fact, it is as tough as it gets, and if you crack the marriage code, it can be the most fulfilling and inspiring of relationships. More satisfying than your relationship with money, friends, food, or the rest of the world.

We usually find a mate in our 20s. If you don't, then your parents find one for you. Either way, you can't really tell if your marriage will work out with that person. The reason for that, I think, is that many people start taking their spouse for granted after the wedding. They feel that this achievement is now complete, and nothing further is needed to be done. That formalising the relationship was the destination. That spouses will give everything to the relationship without expecting anything in return.

Remember: Every relationship is a two-way street. Both partners have to walk towards each other for a relationship to work.

I like to imagine marriage as a separate being, but this being is not self-sustaining and does not survive on its own. It is a being that needs nourishment, a constant supply of food, water, and air to survive and thrive.

A term that is spoken about ubiquitously when it comes to marriage is compatibility. What is it?

Compatibility

Compatibility is the external factor that characterises a relationship. A married couple is like a machine that is part of a bigger machine: the family, which is part of yet another machine: society. Each piece of the machine has to work together for society to function correctly. Compatibility defines if each part can work with the other. If one gear does not fit into the other, the machine will not move. Similarly, if one partner does not fit with the other, the marriage will not work, the family will be troubled, and it will be an anomaly for society.

To be compatible, the partners need not be the same in their understanding of the world, but they need to be similar. They should harmonise with each other so that one partner can understand the other.

Compatibility between two people does not have to be perfect. As long as both partners share the feeling of fitting in, it somehow works. For example, I was more of a sightseeing traveller, and my wife preferred leisure travel. She has no interest in the sites; she would want to relax. She would detest my trip planning, which would usually be packed with a lot of sightseeing and less relaxation. So in one of our travels, I decided to see her point of view and did not plan anything. I just lazed around on the beach with her, and I realised it was not all that bad. In fact, it was wonderful to just relax. And I realised that once we had rested for a few hours or even for a day or two, she would want to go see places. That was the cue, and I started planning our travels to balance relaxing and exploring. The moral of the story is that in many cases (but not all), compatibility is nothing but the art of balancing each other's needs. If a couple can maintain that balance, they are compatible. If they can't, even after trying, they are looking for hard times ahead.

So, some adjustments are needed to have a new part added to the machine. Still, as long as both partners are ready to move together, the machine works, the partnership works, and it can work wonders. That is how the system of marriage has to work. Each partner has to take the initiative in adapting and moulding. Each partner has to balance their needs, wants, and beliefs with the others.

Compatibility can be seen as extremely complicated or simple. We can cloud our minds with various concepts around compatibility or see it as a straightforward way for two individuals to live together. Some people may say that two people should have a hierarchy for the relationship to work, while others may say that they should move parallelly as friends. The fact is that there is no hard and fast rule. You must follow your gut feeling for each situation you encounter. Sometimes, one partner will need to empower himself or herself and take a stand or a decision that might not sit well with the other partner, and sometimes both partners will need to decide mutually and be more like friends. Every situation will require different handling. As long as both partners have an underlying respect for each other and each person is dealing with life situations with awareness, the rest of the things will take care of themselves.

We all have heard that the most essential requirement for a marriage to work is communication. I do not deny that, but I have my own list of priorities that I believe is necessary for a healthy marriage.

Communication

Open and honest communication is the bedrock of a strong marriage. Partners must be willing to share their thoughts, feelings, needs, and concerns with each other regularly. This includes both the big things and the little everyday matters. Make time to really talk and listen to one another without distractions.

Good communication isn't just about expressing yourself, but also listening attentively and seeking to understand your partner's perspective. It requires vulnerability, empathy, and respect from both sides. When conflicts arise, approach them as a team, focusing on 'we' rather than 'you vs. me'. Use 'I feel' statements rather than accusations.

Schedule regular check-ins and date nights to keep the lines of communication open. And don't forget the power of non-verbal communication too - a warm smile, a caring touch, or a thoughtful gesture can communicate love and appreciation beyond words. Like anything worthwhile, good communication takes continuous effort and practice. But it is an essential ingredient for building an enduring, fulfilling relationship.

Respect

Respect your partner. If you do not do that already, then learn to respect your partner. For a relationship to work, both partners need to respect each other and value each other's individuality. Understand that each of you is a separate being who has decided to build a family and a life together. If one of you is working, then understand that the other partner is doing the tougher job of managing the house and making it a home. Understand that each of you has different aspirations, needs, wants, and beliefs. Once you have accepted your partner as a separate individual and have learnt to respect your partner's individuality, it is easier to find that balance.

If some of you think you respect your spouse or are ready to respect them, but you do not get respect in return, you need to earn that respect. Both aspects are important: learn to respect your partner and earn the respect you deserve from your partner.

Do not expect unconditional love and respect. That sounds good in the movies. But, in the real-world, expecting something unconditionally is like thinking that social media is free. Nothing is free; nothing is unconditional in the relationship of marriage. Understand one thing, though, it is, in fact, a give-and-get relationship that is different from a give-and-take relationship. In marriage, you get more of what you give. The more love you give, the more love you get; the more respect you give, the more respect you will get; the more anger and hatred you give, the more anger and hatred you will receive.

To receive respect or to be deserving of receiving respect, you first have to respect yourself. If you do not find yourself worthy of respect, it is unlikely that anybody else will. You also need to respect your partner, and that respect cannot be an eyewash. That can happen when you start focusing on the positive aspects of your partner or spouse. How can you focus on the positive aspects? You can do that when your own thoughts are positive. When you start focusing on the positive side of your partner, you also start earning respect for yourself, and that is how you reach the stage of mutual respect. Fake love and respect can last for a few days, months, or even a few years but not for a lifetime.

There will be people who would say that my partner has nothing positive about them. I am not saying that you carry on with the toxic or abusive relationship, looking for the positives. You would be better off outside such a relationship than being in it and trying to make it work. Respect works when you are with a compatible partner. Compatibility cannot be created nor can it be imagined. It works when you are two sides of a coin, not when you are two different currencies altogether.

"ek myaan mein do talavaar nahin rah sakate"

– Hindi Proverb

Two swords do not fit in one sheath

Suppose nothing works and you finally realise that both of you are not compatible when no beliefs match. In that case, it is better to come out of such a relationship. In my personal and professional life, I have observed that it becomes a battle of egos when a marriage is failing. Instead of parting ways, it becomes a fight to the death. How can that be healthy? How can your mind stay positive when you are in a bitter battle of one-upmanship? I have seen that people who would rather get out of such relationships are better off. They can reboot and restart their life instead of wasting precious years in negativity.

With some effort in the right direction, they get over the unpleasant past and start looking forward. However, when you engage in battle over lost time, you lose more time. You get stuck in the past, and there is no bright future to look forward to until one of the fighting forces surrenders. So, be forward-looking and move on. A better life awaits only when you release your present from the prison of the past.

Responsibilities

Marriage comes with its own bundle of responsibilities. You start thinking of financial independence, raising a family, managing the house, managing kids (if and when you decide to have them), managing your social life, managing the families of each other, and so on and so forth.

Suppose one partner were to think that I could take on one responsibility of the household, such as earning money. The rest will be taken care of by my partner. In that case, they are in for a nasty surprise.

As a married person soon realises, money is just one aspect of being in a marriage. Several hats are to be worn simultaneously, and it only works if the responsibilities are shared. It is not a difficult skill to learn, but it does require patience and practice. If you have decided to share your life with someone, be ready to share the burden of responsibilities. There are many aspects of shared households, from seemingly trivial things such as paying utility bills, cooking, cleaning, etc., to more complicated ones such as buying a new house, managing finances, parenting, etc.

When I was younger, I observed that my father had the responsibility of earning money and managing finances. On the other hand, my mother was entirely responsible for managing the household, household chores, and the kids. This led to an imbalance since my father thought my mother's job was less important than his work. In contrast, my mother believed that my father was keeping himself busy unnecessarily and was not doing enough for the family. Unfortunately, this was the scenario in most households while I was growing up.

I, in the middle, had no clue whom to follow as a role model since the roles appeared to be poles apart and set in stone. In my own wisdom, I tasked myself to balance my learnings to manage myself inside the house and in the outside world. Now I feel the importance of having done that. I am more than happy to share work inside and outside the home, maintaining married life smoothly.

Love

Where does love fit in, one may ask, and it is a relevant question. The relationship becomes relevant and lasting when it is based on love, which, over time, transcends into something more profound. When the physical attraction is not enough, and you develop an emotional attraction for your spouse. When sex is not enough, and you feel the need for support from your spouse. The meaning of love changes throughout married life. We usually get married in our 20s; that is when the novelty of this relationship dawns upon us. That is when we experience the difference between knowing a person and living with that person. The difference between the two experiences defines and decides how we feel about love. We also get to know if the two partners are compatible. Everything else follows with constant efforts from both partners. An ongoing effort is required to bring in respect for each other, share responsibilities, support each other's decisions, and not impose your views. This is important even though you may, at some point, feel that your spouse may be taking the wrong decision. Everyone goes through their own cycle of experiences. You do not learn unless you experience. We can only absorb 5% from the experiences of others; the rest, 95%, is our own experiences. We may learn and course-correct from the teachings of others while we are in that process and path, but what we cannot do is not be on that path based on someone else's experiences.

For a healthy relationship, you will need to emphasise emotional attachment rather than just physical attraction. By being emotionally attached, I mean knowing and understanding how your spouse emotionally reacts in a situation. In a few years of living together, you get a fair idea of that. At different times and circumstances, the intensity of those reactions may change, but the response usually doesn't. Once you know the reaction that will follow a particular situation, you anticipate that reaction and silently provide the support needed. I say silently since if you announce the support you are providing, it loses its value. It comes from within and with time. You only need to be aware and willing to embrace it.

Show Your Love

Feeling love is not enough; you need to make the other person know how you feel. Saying the words to your partner will not be enough; you need to show your love with actions. Actions to show your love will combine both practical and affectionate actions. Utilitarian activities help with household chores. Do not leave them to one partner. You reside in the shared household, so the responsibility to take care of that house is also shared. Pitch in with deliberate and conscious household work. For example, calling in the electrician to get the lights fixed, hanging out the laundry to dry, etc. Get yourself involved, and you will also appreciate the work done by your spouse around the house.

Affectionate actions are more of the physical kind where you show your love for your partner with small nuggets of love throughout the day. For example, hold hands when you can. Call your partner during the day when you know they might be available to take your call to say how much you love them, or just text. Massage your partner's head or feet; it shows both love and respect. These small steps can go a long way in helping you lead a happy and healthy married life.

Healing from Heartbreak

Even the most loving relationships sometimes end, leaving us broken-hearted. The pain of a breakup can be overwhelming - a crushing mix of sadness, anger, rejection, and shattered dreams for the future. In the rawness of heartbreak, it's hard to imagine ever feeling whole again.

Give yourself full permission to grieve. Surround yourself with supportive people who can listen without judgement and remind you of your worth. Find healthy outlets for the intense emotions - talk to a counsellor, write in a journal, move your body. Resist the temptation to numb the pain with drugs, alcohol, or rebound relationships.

Be patient and compassionate with yourself. Healing is a gradual process that can't be rushed. Some days will feel like progress, others like you're back at square one. That's normal. Trust that, with time and tender self-care, the intensity of this pain will subside.

When you're ready, look for the growth opportunities embedded in this experience. What did this relationship teach you about yourself, your needs, your boundaries? How can you emerge from this a stronger, wiser version of yourself? A breakup or a divorce is an ending, but it's also the start of a new story.

Reach out to the things that ground you and give you joy outside of a relationship. Reconnect with friends, hobbies, and goals you may have neglected. Rebuild your identity as an individual, remembering that you are whole and worthy with or without a partner.

Heartbreak cracks us open, allowing us to love ourselves and others more authentically. With support and self-compassion, this painful chapter can transform into a bridge towards a new beginning and a love that will be the right fit.

Conclusion

Relationships, and particularly the deep bond of marriage, are among the most profound and transformative experiences of human life. Through our intimate connections with others, we have the opportunity to love, grow, and discover ourselves in ways that are impossible to achieve alone. By cultivating the skills and virtues of healthy relationships, we can create a foundation of love, trust, and partnership that enriches every aspect of our lives.

At the heart of any strong relationship is a commitment to communication, empathy, and understanding. This means learning to listen deeply, express ourselves authentically, and navigate conflicts with patience, respect, and a willingness to find common ground. It means being attuned to the needs, desires, and perspectives of our partners and working together to create a shared vision of the life and love we want to build.

Another key aspect of nurturing relationships is maintaining a sense of individuality and personal growth. While it's natural and beautiful to merge our lives with our partners, it's equally important to preserve our own sense of self, interests, and purpose. By encouraging each other's passions, supporting each other's dreams, and giving each other space to grow and explore, we create a dynamic and evolving partnership that is always fresh and alive.

In the context of marriage, this balance of togetherness and individuality takes on even greater significance. As we navigate the joys and challenges of building a life together – from managing finances and households to raising children and facing life's inevitable ups and downs – it's essential to approach our partnership with intentionality, adaptability, and a spirit of teamwork. By cultivating habits of appreciation, forgiveness, and renewed commitment, we can weather any storm and emerge stronger, wiser, and more deeply in love.

Ultimately, the art of relationships and married life is about learning to love fully, bravely, and unconditionally. It's about choosing to see the best in our partners, even in moments of frustration or disappointment. It's about being willing to be vulnerable, to take risks, and to grow together through the seasons of life. It's about creating a sanctuary of love, laughter, and belonging that allows us to be our truest, most authentic selves.

The beauty of mastering relationships and marriage is that it has a ripple effect on every other area of our lives. When we feel loved, supported, and cherished by our partners, we show up in the world with greater confidence, creativity, and generosity of spirit. We become better parents, friends, colleagues, and community members, spreading the love and lessons we've learnt in our most intimate relationships.

Whether you are currently in a relationship, married, or seeking a future partner, remember that the key to lasting love lies in the daily choices and actions that shape your connection. Choose to prioritise your relationship, to invest in open and loving communication, and to never stop growing and discovering each other anew.

Relationships and married life are not just about finding happiness, but about creating it, day by day, moment by moment. They are about building a legacy of love that endures through the generations and modelling for others what it means to love and be loved in return. By embracing the art of relationships with courage, compassion, and a commitment to lifelong learning, we open ourselves up to the greatest adventure and reward of human life – the journey of the heart.

Parenting

There is no such thing as a perfect parent. So just be a real one.

– Sue Atkins

I think all parents would agree that parenting is hard. No wonder, in the legal jargon, the word for a child is 'issue'. The good thing is it comes naturally to parents. We all want the best for our children. The problem is that our idea of what is best for our children differs based on our own conditioning, ideas, thoughts, and upbringing. Without even noticing, we end up imposing our beliefs and opinions on our kids only because we can.

When it comes to bringing up kids, my idea is to curb my natural instinct, which might be conditioned by my past, and think of kids as individual beings; separate human beings with their own set of likes, dislikes, tastes, ambitions, and aspirations. My job as a parent is not to mould my kids in my own image but only to mentor and guide them based on their individuality. I have to allow them to live their own lives. That is a tough job to do as a parent. It is easy to forget this principle and lead them on a path that follows yours. But, that is because we have already created that path. We know the track, the potholes, speed breakers, and traffic lights on that path.

The questions we start asking ourselves are: If nature has attached responsibility to me for my children, and they are on another path, how much guidance will I be able to give? How much will I be able to help them? Will I be able to help them? These are the wrong questions since they only mean one thing: I am trying to control my child's life.

My role as a parent is not to be in the driver's seat but only to lead my child to the driver's seat. I can't do the driving, not even backseat driving. I can only teach the ropes: holding the steering, using the indicators, and seeing what is coming behind you and what's ahead of you. Then, once they have learnt those skills, I want to sit back, observe, and guide them when needed.

How can you do that?

- Lead by example
- Be flexible
- Understand your child's individuality and let it flourish
- Think like a guide/teacher

Lead by Example

Kids, especially younger ones, will not understand your explanation of right or wrong or acceptable or unacceptable behaviour, but they observe and learn. If they are in an environment of violence, they will take violence as the acceptable way of life. Similarly, if they are in an atmosphere of love and cooperation, they will consider those values to be universal truths and imbibe them. Needless to say, the first ground of learning is the family. In a family replete with violence or animosity between family members, the child, no matter how well you may try to shield them, will either take to violence as an expression of their being or will be full of fear. Either of these will prevent the child from engaging with the world fully.

In other words, the child will be prevented from living life to the fullest. These values, which the child learns from observation, are not just random, intermittent observations, but constant observation that instils unwavering faith in those values in the young child's mind. For the child, that particular value, whether good or bad, is the ultimate reality. Therefore, if the child lives in an environment of constant love, support, cooperation, and respect, the child will pick up those habits and values. If a child is looking at her parents exercising every day, she would know and believe that exercising is a good thing that should be done. The children trust their caretakers and thrive in the safety of their guardians. If the guardian is feeling unsafe, could the one who is guarded feel safe? The child will be living in fear and will partake in the same fears as her parents.

Now imagine the following situation. You indulge in unhealthy eating, the sodas, chips, fries and the works, and then you ask your child not to eat junk food; what do you think the child will believe? Suppose she sees her father shouting, or in the worst of cases, hitting her mother. How strong, do you think, would be the child's belief in the concept of love or in the institution of marriage? That is why you have to lead by example. If you want your child to be healthy, make healthy choices yourself. If you want your child to be friendly, choose to be sociable and cooperative. If you want your child to be happy, choose to be happy yourself. Let the child watch and learn and implement all the values you wish for her to absorb in her life.

Be Flexible

As a parent, we cannot be rigid. We can't bind ourselves to one approach or method of parenting. We need to trust our intuition and work accordingly. By the time he was two and a half years old, my younger son was highly volatile and aggressive. His first reaction to every situation that he was averse to was hitting the other person, and if he was stopped, then he would hit me or cry out loud. At that stage, he could not comprehend any reasoning I might offer for not behaving in a particular manner. I tried offering rewards for good behaviour, but that did not work. To make him understand the consequences of his actions, I would reprimand him or discipline him by making him sit alone in a room for a few minutes. Now, even though the room may have things to play with, he would quickly realise that he has not been let inside the room to play. He would shout to come out. This is when I would calm him down, explain to him, and teach him to say sorry. Initially, he did not understand its meaning, but he did take 'sorry' to be some magic word.

The purpose was not just to teach him to say sorry but to improve and mould his behaviour. The trips to the room happened at least twice every week. Sometimes, I deliberately ignored his aggressive actions because I did not want the discipline to become so frequent that it lost its value. At these times, I could see that he felt relieved for not being reprimanded. That meant that he was getting to understand which actions were acceptable and which were not.

Within a month, I could see a change. I saw my son pick up his hands to hit but stopping in his tracks, realising the consequences. At this time, I cut down on disciplining him, but I started explaining the need for good behaviour. Every time he hit or tried to hit his sister, I would explain to him that he had made a mistake and then make him say sorry and give her a hug. Soon, he understood what actions were acceptable and which ones were not. I taught him that hitting someone, even playfully, is never an option, and tickling is a more fun option that everyone can enjoy. This way, I redirected his energies to a more acceptable action.

With time, he learnt to control his actions, redirecting his energies, and he also learnt to share with others. Once that happened, I changed my strategy and instead started reinforcing that he was a good and caring boy. At one point in time, I started calling him Mr Good Boy, and he would respond by saying, "Yes, I am a good boy." The concept of acceptable behaviour had been entrenched in him by now. Maybe he felt it essential to keep up with his good boy image, especially since it came with many perks. He aligned his behaviour with his belief, and that could be seen in his actions. All of this took about a year.

Once, when I was working on something from home, I heard a loud noise of toys being thrown around his room while he played with a friend. I went to check in, and before I could say anything, he said, "Sorry, Papa! You will not hear more noise." I felt relieved and satisfied. Therefore, one approach does not fit every child, nor is it suitable at every point in time. Every situation needs to be worked on differently, and you will need to think of novel ways to connect with your children.

<u>Understand Your Child's Individuality and Let It Flourish</u>

We already know that each person is different. As we grow up, we start wearing masks to fit in with the world. Those masks take away a lot of our individuality. However, that is not the case with children. Children wear their individuality. They do not have a code to live by. As parents, we need to honour their identity, and we can do that by letting it flourish. It is not difficult to understand the personality of a child. It is always out in the open; we only need to observe.

When my daughter was two, I started reading stories to her during bedtime, and she would listen with intent. There was never a day when I wouldn't read a story to her. I could see, from a very early age, that she was creative and imaginative. I wanted her imagination to flourish. We used to play a game where we would imagine some environment and act out our roles in those surroundings. For example, while sitting on the couch, I would ask her to imagine we were on an aeroplane. I would be the pilot, and she would describe what she could see as we flew around.

Now she is eight, an avid reader, extraordinarily creative, and with a vivid imagination. That can also be seen from the creative writing and story writing work that she does at school.

On the other hand, until he was three and a half, my son had no interest in stories or books. Even if he picked up a book himself and brought it to me to read to him, he would become disinterested within one minute and start fidgeting. However, one fine day, his interest in bedtime stories arose, and now he listens to at least two stories every night. He is more outgoing, interested in physical activities. His toys of choice are cars. My playtime with him involves jumping and running around. It is already clear that his personality is different, and I would need to shift gears for each of them.

There cannot be a blanket method of parenting that applies to all except love. No matter the personality type, every child is receptive to love. Don't keep that love in your head; show it to your kids, in your actions and in your words. Make time for them. If you do that, things and toys will not matter. You will not need to bribe them to listen to you. Children are incredibly receptive to love. If they feel that love, they will listen to you and understand you. Love is the true parenting language.

Think Like a Guide or Teacher

As children grow older and move into the outside world, they will engage with the world like a butterfly. As a caterpillar, they were confined to a small space and are now going out and about. There is so much for them to see and explore. It's a transition for the kids and the parents since we become comfortable with a certain way our kids behave. We have developed a strategy for working with the kids. The teenage years, during which the transition happens, are not easy, either for the kids or the parents. That is because, as parents, we have gotten used to a particular way of life, and it is difficult to change it. But, on the other hand, for teenagers, change is the only option. Their relationship with the world is changing, and they have no idea what to expect.

During this time, you will need two things in abundance: love and patience. As parents, we will undoubtedly be anxious and fearful. However, we will need to rearrange the blocks to make a larger circle within which our children will move around and engage with the world. As parents, the first instinct might be to stop them or restrict them, which would be the wrong approach. Instead, we should endeavour to engage with the kids and enjoy the amazement as they explore the unseen. The difference is that, as parents, we would want to oversee and instruct based on our assessment of what they are going through. As guides, we will move with them, learning about their experiences. Since we will be moving with them and learning with them, we will guide them to the right course wherever needed.

Children will allow you to accompany them on their journeys only if you are receptive to their way of thinking. That can happen only with positive and constructive communication. When you listen to them with intent, they will be receptive to what you have to say. If you only instruct, they will be quick to ignore you and chart their own path. Communication is the key.

Going back to the car analogy, children do not need an instructor; they may do well with the navigator by their side. Never forget that love and compassion trump everything else.

<u>Remember:</u>

- Spend more time with your kids instead of money.
- Make your child feel loved at every available opportunity.
- Use positive words and language around them.
- Praise them often.
- If you are busy and children seek your attention, do not ignore them or scold them. Instead, try to explain your need for some disturbance-free time. Then, nine out of ten times, they will understand.
- Do not worry if they do not stick to one hobby or activity. Instead, let them explore different things and make-up their own mind over time.
- The two most important habits you can help your child develop are reading and exercise.
- More than anything else, be patient with them.

Conclusion

Parenting is perhaps the most challenging, rewarding, and transformative journey of human life. From the moment a child enters our world, we are forever changed – not just in our daily routines and responsibilities, but in the very fabric of our hearts and souls. As parents, we have the sacred privilege and duty of shaping the next generation, of guiding our children towards lives of meaning, purpose, and contribution.

At its core, effective parenting is about providing our children with the love, security, and guidance they need to thrive. It's about creating a home environment that is nurturing, stimulating, and responsive to their unique needs and personalities. It's about setting clear boundaries and expectations, while also allowing our children the freedom to explore, make mistakes, and discover their own paths.

One of the key aspects of positive parenting is emotional attunement and connection. By learning to read and respond to our children's emotional cues, we help them develop a strong sense of self, empathy, and resilience. We teach them that their feelings matter and that they can turn to us for comfort, guidance, and support. Through daily rituals of play, conversation, and affection, we build a foundation of trust and attachment that will carry them through life's challenges.

Another crucial component of parenting is modelling the values, skills, and behaviours we wish to instil in our children. Children learn far more from what we do than what we say, and they are constantly absorbing the lessons of our example. By striving to live with integrity, compassion, and a growth mindset, we give our children a powerful template for their own lives. By admitting our own mistakes and limitations, we teach them the value of humility, forgiveness, and lifelong learning.

Beyond the day-to-day practicalities of parenting, it's also essential to cultivate a long-term vision for our children's development and well-being. This means being intentional about the experiences, opportunities, and relationships we provide for them and advocating for their needs and potential in the wider world. It means helping them develop the skills of critical thinking, creativity, and adaptability that will serve them in a rapidly changing future. It means nurturing their unique gifts and passions while also preparing them for the responsibilities and challenges of adulthood.

Ultimately, the art of parenting is about learning to let go, even as we hold on. It's about recognising that our children are not extensions of ourselves, but separate and sovereign beings with their own destinies to fulfil. As they grow and change, so too must our roles and relationships evolve – from hands-on caregivers to wise mentors, from constant companions to trusted advisers. The greatest gift we can give our children is not a life free from struggle, but the tools and resilience to navigate whatever challenges come their way.

The beauty of embracing the journey of parenthood is that it has the power to transform not just our children, but ourselves. Through the daily demands and delights of raising a child, we are called to grow in patience, empathy, and unconditional love. We are challenged to confront our own limitations and fears and to model the kind of adulthood we hope our children will one day embody. In the end, parenting is not just about raising healthy, happy children, but about becoming our best selves in the process.

So, to all the parents out there, remember that you are doing the most important work of your lives. You are shaping the future, one precious child at a time. Trust in your instincts, lean on your community, and never stop learning and growing alongside your children.

Parenting is the ultimate adventure – a journey of love, discovery, and transformation that lasts a lifetime. Embrace it with all your heart and know that the seeds you plant today will bear fruit for generations to come. That is the extraordinary privilege and responsibility of being a parent.

Health

"Sar salamat toh pagadi hazaar."

– Hindi proverb

If your head is intact, you can have a thousand turbans.

Could I do anything at all if my body is not cooperating? Of course not. A healthy body is a prerequisite and a necessity for moving anywhere, doing anything, and achieving anything. Generally speaking, in our 20s, the body's metabolism is high, energy levels are better, and overall health is optimum. In our 30s, the metabolism takes a nosedive, energy levels are lower, and our health may deteriorate unless we take proper care.

By proper care, I do not mean spending a few hours every week at the gym. I suggest maintaining optimum health through regular, moderate exercise and making improvements in diet. Exercising is one part of health. However, indulging in a healthy lifestyle is more important, and for that, what we consume becomes all the more important. I understand that overall health is 70% of what we consume and 30% of what we do with our bodies.

Just a few years back, there was a time when late-night snacking was the norm, especially when watching TV, which I also did a lot. There was no control over the things I was consuming, be it fried or processed food and sugary drinks. Exercising was an option that I did not take. Before I could understand the implications of my unhealthy lifestyle, my weight had zoomed to 96.5 kg. It was only then that it dawned on me that I could reach a hundred kilograms soon. That thought hit me hard, and I decided to do something about it. From then on, I have tried different things to improve my health, including exercising, diet control, and management.

I started by getting up a little early and going to the park for a walk. After some time, I began adding some running to my walking routine. Over time, I incorporated some exercises as well. Overall, I was exercising for 45 to 60 minutes, 3 to 4 times a week. I was exercising regularly, but I had not changed my diet or my late-night eating habits. After a year, I had improved my fitness levels, but I could only bring my weight down to ninety kgs. It was then that I started making changes to my diet. I found that fad diets such as the GM diet were unimpressive since the weight returned. After a lot of experimentation, I realised there was a simple, methodical way of improving my health and fitness levels.

What my trials and errors have led me to believe are the following tips and tricks for overall health and fitness:

- Get 30 minutes of moderate to intermediate exercise four times a week. This could be in the form of walking, running or a mix of both, sports activities, full-body workouts or dancing, anything that makes you move your body.
- Cut down on processed sugar. Natural sugar substitutes such as jaggery are better alternatives.
- If you smoke, quit.
- Increase intake of raw or steamed fruits and vegetables
- Eat your last meal three hours before bedtime. If you sleep at 10 PM, do not eat anything after 7 PM. If you feel hungry after that, then do something to divert your attention. The following activities are effective:

  - Go for a walk
  - Drink a hot beverage such as green tea or lemon tea
  - Call up a friend
  - Read a book or magazine.
  - Drink water

- Sleep on time. Resting your body is as vital as working it out. You need 6 to 8 hours of sleep every day, and every individual's needs are different, but 6 to 8 hours is the thumb rule. Do the following to improve your sleep:

o   Exercise regularly
o   Go to sleep at a similar time every night
o   Drink a hot caffeine-free beverage before bedtime
o   Relax your body and mind by meditating for 15 to 20 minutes before sleeping
o   Do not drink caffeinated drinks after 6 PM.
o   Soak your feet in warm saline water for 10-15 minutes

If you follow just these few simple things, you are bound to improve your health for the better. Moreover, when the body starts feeling good, it wants to do more of whatever makes it feel good. Thus, you will develop a habit of taking care of your health which offers lifelong benefits. Of course, I am giving you some general tips for improving your physical health, which may work for most. Still, if you have any health issues, you will do yourself a favour by consulting your doctor or a specialist.

If you feel that you will not follow all these together, pick up just one habit to start. I would suggest that you do not eat anything after 7 PM. Then, after a couple of weeks, add another healthy habit of exercising for 30 minutes, three to four times a week. Next, start drinking more water. After that, eat more fruits and veggies.

By applying these tips, I have been able to improve my physical health tremendously. The overall energy levels remain high throughout the day, and I do not avoid physical activity at any point in the day. I have also been able to reduce my weight by about 15 kg.

There are numerous other ways and things that you can incorporate into your lifestyle for better health. I have not covered every aspect here; I can't. But if you follow just these simple principles, you will see excellent results in a few weeks.

Conclusion

Health is the foundation upon which all other aspects of our lives are built. It is the precious gift that allows us to pursue our dreams, enjoy our relationships, and make a positive impact on the world around us. By prioritising our physical, mental, and emotional well-being, we create the conditions for a life of vitality, resilience, and fulfilment.

At the heart of optimal health is a commitment to self-care and preventive medicine. This means taking proactive steps to nourish our bodies with wholesome foods, regular exercise, and restful sleep. It means managing stress through techniques like meditation, deep breathing, and time in nature. It means cultivating a positive mindset and healthy relationships that support our overall well-being. By making these practices a daily priority, we build a strong foundation of health that can withstand life's challenges.

Another key aspect of health is being an informed and empowered advocate for our own care. This means educating ourselves about our bodies, our risk factors, and the latest advances in medical science. It means partnering with healthcare professionals who listen to our concerns, respect our values, and work collaboratively to optimise our health. It means being proactive about screenings, vaccinations, and preventive treatments that can catch and address health issues early. By taking an active role in our healthcare, we can make informed decisions that align with our unique needs and goals.

Beyond individual self-care, creating a culture of health also requires addressing the social, economic, and environmental factors that shape our collective well-being. This means advocating for policies and practices that promote health equity, such as access to affordable healthcare, healthy food, and safe living conditions. It means recognising the interconnectedness of our health with the health of our communities and our planet, and taking action to create a more just and sustainable world. By working together to build a culture of health, we create the conditions for all people to thrive.

Ultimately, the path to optimal health is a lifelong journey of learning, growth, and self-discovery. It requires patience, persistence, and a willingness to adapt to the changing needs of our bodies and minds over time. It means embracing both the joys and the challenges of taking care of ourselves and recognising that our health is not just an end in itself but a means to living a life of purpose and meaning.

The beauty of prioritising our health is that it has a ripple effect on every other aspect of our lives. When we feel energised, resilient, and centred, we show up more fully in our relationships, our work, and our communities. We have the vitality and clarity to pursue our passions, face our fears, and make a positive difference in the world. By investing in our health, we create a powerful legacy of well-being that extends far beyond ourselves.

Wherever you are on your health journey, remember that every small step matters. Every choice to nourish your body, calm your mind, and connect with others is a powerful act of self-love and self-care. Trust in your body's innate wisdom, seek out the support and resources you need, and never stop learning and growing.

Health is not just the absence of disease, but the presence of vitality, resilience, and joy. It is the foundation for a life well-lived and the greatest gift we can give ourselves and those we love. By embracing the art of health, we open ourselves up to a world of limitless possibility and potential. And that is the essence of a life in full bloom.

Death and Loss

This is a complex topic to discuss but an important one, nonetheless. Let's face it, by the mid-30s, most of us realise we do not have a lifetime ahead of us. That's how we had felt in our teens. The twenties are too busy a time to actually sit down and think. In our 30s, we realise how time flies, and then we start questioning our choices and if, so far, we have used our time on Earth wisely. Many of us think about changes, but most of us are unable to go past our thinking and bring it into action. The thought of change remains just that, a thought. By the mid-30s, we start thinking that we have reached midlife or are almost there; now, we should get things going before it's too late. We dwell on the urgency and also contemplate the futility of it all. The far-fetched concept of death appears a little closer.

Death is life's great leveller. No matter what you have done or not done, achieved or not achieved, no one can avoid the inevitability of death. You can, of course, take steps to increase your life expectancy by paying more attention to your physical and mental health. However, it is just that, an expectancy since death cannot be predicted.

If nothing much can be done about it, why are we discussing it here?

Well, I think that the end can help us enjoy the journey more. Knowing about the unavoidability of death can help us live our lives better.

Consider that you are stuck in a bad situation, maybe in your job or relationship, and then consider how you would have dealt with it if you were aware that you do not have much time left on Earth, that the end is not too far.

That awareness would help you evaluate the situation afresh. Your newly found viewpoint may give you the perspective on the situation that you may not have considered otherwise. As a result, you will be able to make better choices. You get the superpower to assess what is important for you to invest your time and energy in life. The thought of impending death is like that bitter medicine you want to avoid taking, but it can help you recover much faster once you do.

A small amount of time to think about death once in a while could give you a new lease of life. 'Lease of life' is a perfect phrase for the concept of life and death since we are all on borrowed time on Earth. What is it that will matter when my time comes? Is it wealth, job, name and fame, family, or children? Will any of the grudges you hold against others matter? You will realise that nothing will matter. You will be gone, and whatever is left on Earth will remain. Your family, children, relatives will move their own course and experience their own lives.

When we accept the impermanence of life, we can love, work, and play with renewed energy to make our time on Earth count. Never assume that you have the whole life ahead of you. Whatever you have is here, now. No one can predict what is going to happen in the next moment. So do not wait for another time to show your love, to show your respect, to bury your grudges, to forgive and forget. Do not wait to live your life; there may not be another time.

There is a downside to this as well. While embracing the inevitability of death frees us, the fear of death confines us. In the book 'Homo Deus: A Brief History of Tomorrow', Yuval Noah Harari touches upon the topic of how some wealthy individuals are trying to find a death cure, a way to achieve immortality. Till now, science has been able to prolong lives by reducing premature deaths. Cheating death by prolonging the typical lifespan of human beings sounds like science fiction but is being undertaken by some companies. Biotechnology is advancing, but it is hard to say if, when, and how immortality will be achieved and the consequences for our already distressed planet.

Coming back to the present, if you think about death too often and ponder on it too much, it may have the opposite effect. Instead of becoming more joyful of life, of the present moment, we can become more fearful of death. Instead of using our time productively, we could consider everything futile and resign to a life of insignificance.

To avoid such a situation, our contemplation of death must always be followed by gratitude for our life. Being aware of the possibility of death should not make you fearful but should push you to improve your life. This can happen if you realise the importance of receiving the gift of life and a thinking mind. Be grateful for this life. To experience the beauty of life is a gift. Appreciate its value. Be present in the present, and you will be able to come out of the cycle of regrets.

The above exercise will save you from regrets when the time actually arrives. It will help you take steps in the right direction, make better decisions, show more affection to your loved ones, and generally be more upbeat about this short life that we have on Earth.

This is your own life which you can mould by directing your thoughts. What about the situations that are not under your control when you experience the loss of a loved one?

All of us have lived through a pandemic recently, something none of us had imagined could happen, but the larger reality does not care about our individual imagination. We saw a lot of deaths and losses around us. There is a real fear, and that is affecting every aspect of our lives. Since death is inevitable, the loss of a loved one is unavoidable. No matter how much we might want to avoid thinking about it, we cannot avoid experiencing loss.

Everyone copes with loss differently, and I feel that the best way to do it is to engage in something constructive. Any activity that will not only keep your mind engaged but will also help in developing a feeling of overcoming and accomplishing something. It could be a hobby you always wanted to pursue, learning a new language, starting a new venture, etc. Anything that helps you divert your thoughts to something more constructive will help you overcome the underlying feelings of fear and loss. Taking constructive action has also been discussed in the chapters on Positive Thinking and Mental Health.

Losing a Parent

For many of us, the first profound experience of loss comes with the passing of a parent. Our parents are our anchors, our guiding stars through life. Losing them can feel like the ground has shifted beneath our feet, leaving us unmoored and adrift.

The grief of losing a parent is multilayered. We grieve not only for the person they were but for the role they played in our lives - as a caregiver, adviser, confidante, and unconditional supporter. We may feel like we've lost our compass, our safety net, a piece of our identity.

It's important to allow yourself to fully experience the pain of this loss. Grieve in your own way and on your own timeline. Seek support from others who understand.

At the same time, losing a parent is also a poignant opportunity for growth and transformation. Even as we mourn their absence, we can honour their presence by reflecting on and carrying forward their wisdom, values, and dreams for us. Losing a parent thrusts us into a new phase of adulthood. It challenges us to reorient ourselves, trust our judgement, and define life on our terms.

In a sense, losing a parent is the final step in a long process of individuation that began in adolescence. Though it may feel daunting, it is also an invitation to spread our wings and soar, guided by their love and lessons, which remain forever a part of us.

Conclusion

Death and loss are an inherent part of the human experience, touching every life at some point in the journey. Whether it's the passing of a beloved family member, friend, or pet, or the loss of a cherished relationship, job, or way of life, grief is a universal emotion that binds us together in our shared humanity. By learning to navigate the complex terrain of loss with courage, compassion, and resilience, we can find meaning, healing, and growth even in life's darkest moments.

One of the most profound aspects of experiencing loss is the way it illuminates the preciousness and impermanence of life. In the face of death, we are confronted with the truth that our time on Earth is finite and that every moment, connection, and experience is a fleeting gift to be cherished. This awareness can be both terrifying and liberating, inviting us to live with greater intention, gratitude, and presence. By embracing the reality of our mortality, we can learn to savour the sweetness of life in all its fragile beauty.

Another key aspect of navigating death and loss is allowing ourselves to fully feel and express the pain of grief. Too often, our culture rushes us to 'move on' or 'get over' our losses, minimising the depth and complexity of the grieving process. But grief is not a linear journey with a clear endpoint; it is a winding path that ebbs and flows, sometimes for a lifetime. By honouring our grief and creating space for all its messy, uncomfortable emotions – from anger and despair to confusion and guilt – we slowly integrate our losses into the fabric of our lives, finding new ways to carry our loved ones with us.

In the midst of loss, it's also crucial to reach out for support and connection. Grief can be an isolating experience, making us feel alone and misunderstood in our pain. But by sharing our stories, memories, and emotions with others who have experienced similar losses, we can find comfort, validation, and a sense of belonging. Whether it's through therapy, support groups, or heart-to-heart conversations with friends and family, surrounding ourselves with a network of love and understanding can make all the difference in our healing journey.

Ultimately, the path through death and loss is a deeply personal and transformative one. It asks us to confront the most profound questions of existence – about the nature of life and death, the meaning of suffering, and the enduring power of love. It invites us to grapple with our own beliefs about what lies beyond this earthly plane and to find ways to honour and stay connected to those we have lost. In the crucible of grief, we are forever changed, broken open to new depths of compassion, resilience, and appreciation for the sacred gift of life.

The beauty of embracing the journey of loss is that it can catalyse tremendous growth and awakening. In the darkness of our pain, we often discover hidden reserves of strength, creativity, and purpose. We learn to live with a more open and grateful heart, knowing that every moment is a precious opportunity for love and connection. We become more attuned to the pain of others and more committed to creating a world of greater kindness, justice, and healing. In the end, the lessons of loss become our greatest teachers, guiding us towards a life of deeper meaning and wisdom.

To all those navigating the uncharted waters of grief, remember that you are not alone. Your pain is a testament to the depth of your love, and your courage in facing it is a powerful act of resilience. Trust in the wisdom of your own heart, lean on the support of others, and know that even in the darkest of times, the light of love and hope still shines.

Death and loss remind us of the sacredness and fragility of this human adventure. They call us to live with greater presence, compassion, and connection, knowing that every moment is a gift to be cherished. By embracing the journey of grief with an open heart, we honour the love that binds us, the memories that sustain us, and the enduring spirit that lives on within us all. And that is the greatest tribute we can pay to those we have lost.

Declutter

Out of clutter, find simplicity.

– Albert Einstein

Imagine you are going on a month-long vacation or for a month-long work trip. You pick up the most enormous suitcase you have available and pack all the stuff you think you will need. You check your baggage weight, and it weighs 40 kg. You check your tickets and realise that your airline allows only 20 kg of baggage. What would you do? You will have two options: you will either have to pay more for carrying more or reassess your needs and take out all the stuff you thought you needed that is really not that essential. Even though by force, you will cut down on 50% of your needs and still enjoy your vacation or survive your work travel.

This transaction applies to life too. Negative thoughts and emotions are heavy; the more we carry, the more we will have to pay. Reduce the weight of these negative emotions; you will feel lighter and will be able to enjoy your life better. Positive thoughts and feelings have the opposite effect; the more you have, the more ethereal you will feel.

Just like our minds, which we fill up with unnecessary thoughts, we fill up our living spaces, our home, and office with unnecessary things. So, just as we need to clean up our minds, we need to clean out our living spaces of useless and unnecessary things.

Clean and decluttered surroundings help us think better. For example, we need a clean office table to think clearly and be more productive, and a clean house to feel rested and comfortable after the day's work.

A decluttered space is also easier to clean. A clean living space helps you stay calm and relaxed. Such a space also makes you want to keep it clean, making you conscious and appreciative of your environment.

Like everything else, decluttering and cleaning also require consistency. If you do not clean your house for a week or two, you cannot hope that it will be spick and span in an hour. So set up a decluttering schedule to maintain consistency. For example, you can set a reminder on your phone for the last Saturday of every quarter. Then, when the day arrives, collect and remove all unnecessary things from the house.

Start with collecting things that have not been used in the last six months, things that are not in working condition, and you have never bothered to have repaired. Chances are that you have already replaced that product or it is no longer needed. Also, find things that were of use earlier but have lost relevance now.

Old technology is an example of that. I can imagine some people still holding on to their fax machines and CD players. It is time to get rid of them.

Another thing that can be done to declutter is to create less clutter and waste. Keep your things, appliances, and equipment maintained with regular servicing. Repair whatever you can.

You will experience that with the disposal of each such item, you will feel lighter and better within. You will start feeling decluttered inside and out.

Conclusion

In a world that often equates success and happiness with the accumulation of material possessions, the act of decluttering can be a radical and transformative choice. By intentionally letting go of the things that no longer serve us – whether physical, emotional, or mental – we create space for what truly matters and align our lives with our deepest values and desires.

At its core, decluttering is about reclaiming our time, energy, and attention from the excess that weighs us down. It's about simplifying our surroundings and our schedules so that we can focus on the people, activities, and experiences that bring us genuine joy and fulfilment. By releasing the clutter in our lives, we also declutter our minds, making room for greater clarity, creativity, and peace.

One of the key benefits of decluttering is the sense of lightness and freedom it brings. When we are no longer burdened by the physical and psychological weight of unnecessary possessions, we feel more agile, adaptable, and open to new possibilities. We are less attached to the past, less anxious about the future, and more fully present in the now. This newfound spaciousness allows us to approach life with greater spontaneity, curiosity, and ease.

Another powerful aspect of decluttering is the way it reflects and reinforces our personal growth. As we evolve and change over time, so do our needs, preferences, and priorities. By regularly reassessing what we own and why, we ensure that our surroundings are a true reflection of who we are in the present moment. We learn to let go of the things that once defined us, making space for the new identities and experiences that are calling us forward.

Beyond the personal benefits, decluttering also has important social and environmental implications. By consuming less and letting go of excess, we reduce our ecological footprint and contribute to a more sustainable future. By donating or repurposing items we no longer need, we support our local communities and help others meet their basic needs. In this way, decluttering becomes an act of generosity and social responsibility, reminding us of our interconnectedness and the impact of our choices.

Ultimately, the practice of decluttering is a lifelong journey of self-discovery and intentional living. It requires us to confront our deepest beliefs about what we need to be happy, secure, and worthy, and to challenge the cultural messages that equate abundance with accumulation. It invites us to redefine success on our own terms and to cultivate a sense of enoughness in a world that constantly tells us we need more.

The beauty of embracing a decluttered life is that it creates the conditions for true abundance to emerge. When we let go of the excess, we make room for the things that truly nourish and sustain us – deeper relationships, meaningful work, creative pursuits, and moments of awe and wonder. We discover that the greatest treasures in life are not things, but experiences, connections, and the beauty of the present moment.

As you embark on your own decluttering journey, remember that the goal is not perfection, but progress. Start small, be patient with yourself, and trust in the wisdom of your own heart. Surround yourself with supportive people who share your values and celebrate each step forward as a victory.

Decluttering is about choosing a life of intention, authenticity, and joy. It's about aligning our outer world with our inner truth and creating the space for our highest potential to unfold. By letting go of the things that hold us back, we open ourselves up to a world of limitless possibility and abundance. And that is the greatest gift we can give ourselves and the world.

➤ The Thirties Reboot ◄

things that hold us back, we open ourselves up to a world of limitless possibility and abundance. And that is the greatest gift we can give ourselves and the world.

Saying No

"Jab tavaqqo hi uth gayi ghalib
kyun kisi ka gila kare koi."

– Mirza Ghalib (1797-1869)

When there are no expectations,

Why would someone complain?

Saying no is a skill that can save you a whole lot of time and a whole lot of trouble. There are many instances when we agree with someone or agree to do something, not because we want to do it, but only because we do not want the other person to think badly of us. We want to look helpful. We feel that it is a societal burden that we have to bear.

It does not matter if our act is appreciated or not. We do not dare to say no. The reasons for saying yes to things we do not really want to do are:

- Our need for acceptance and admiration
- Our own insecurities

We want to feel loved and admired. In the process of wanting to be loved and respected, we feel that by saying yes, even to things we are uncomfortable doing, we are helping out. In return, we will get the love and admiration we desire.

Unfortunately, this strategy does not work. You end up saying yes to everything as a habit, hoping that this would turn around with the next yes, but it doesn't. For example, your colleague comes to you for help with his presentation; you have enough on your plate, yet you say yes. Take another example: your long-lost friend comes to you in need of money. You know this money will never be returned, and yet you end up saying yes. You may convince yourself that you are helping them by making your own reasons. The only real reason would be that you want to please them to experience acceptance for your actions.

We are creatures of habit. Suppose we have been saying yes to everything, we will end up saying yes even though we know we are not getting any respect, love, or admiration in return. As a result, we may end up losing our time, energy, and money in the process.

People take your yes, your help, for granted. People start expecting you to say yes, for you to go out of the way for them. People will not factor in your agreeing to something as a possibility but an expectation. And when something is an expectation, it is seen as a right and not an exception. In the process, you end up losing the most essential perishable commodity, that is time, with nothing to show for it.

I am not saying that you should never say yes to anything ever. And I am not saying you should not help out wherever needed. All I am saying is that the need of the other person should be genuine. Your help should not come from a feeling of disadvantage, from weakness, from habit, but should come from a sense of strength and advantage. Support is not given to satisfy your ego but to give you inner satisfaction, a feeling of joy that comes from providing help. If you are not joyful helping out someone, you have probably said yes to something you should ideally have said no to.

If you are experiencing the feeling of joy from helping someone, you have made the right decision. But, on the other hand, if you feel that you are being taken advantage of, you are probably correct. It is the latter that you want to avoid. You know that it is not difficult to separate the wheat from the chaff, to distinguish genuine requests from the fake ones. You only need to learn the correct ways to say no without coming across as apathetic or egotistic.

If you have been saying yes for a long time, it will take some time to learn to say no. However, it is a skill that can save you a lot of time and trouble. It will also save you a lot of self-loathing since once you have done something against your will, only because you did not know how to say no, and you have not received whatever you were expecting in return, such as the attention, love, or admiration, you will feel that you have been taken advantage of, and you will curse yourself for it.

Next time, you will end up going through the same cycle as if it is not in your control. It will take effort and skill to break the cycle. That frustration will likely be released on someone else, such as a family member or a junior colleague, which is not an appropriate scenario. You will undoubtedly need a release for your negative thoughts at that stage. Try writing down your thoughts instead of lashing out at someone, including yourself. That will empower you, and your subconscious will tell you what to do. You will not feel helpless or a slave to your habit. Some of the following tips and tricks for saying no may help:

<u>It is my policy:</u> When you say it, as a rule, the other person does not feel that they are being singled out. For example, if an acquaintance asks for money, you may say that my policy is not to lend money to people I know. When you say it as a general policy, you are not separating out that particular individual, and that prevents the person from feeling that they, in particular, have been declined. You do not need to give an explanation of your policy. It is implied and understandable that you have been bitten before.

<u>It is not a good time:</u> Another thing you can say is that it is not a good time right now. This would give the impression that you are willing to help, but you are going through something in your own life or work that prevents you from taking up the task being asked of you.

As a bonus, saying no will also help you gain confidence, and you will be in more control of yourself, your time, and your life.

The following points should be kept in mind when informing about your decision:

Be Polite but Firm

You do not have to come across as rude, and at the same time, you do not have to present a chance or possibility that you might agree. Do not leave that window open to allow the other person to let themselves in. For example, if you say, "Maybe I am not the right person for this," the person asking might persuade you to agree to try out. Instead, if you say, "I am afraid I have other commitments," you will sound polite yet firm.

Avoid being rude, instead be empathetic and appreciative. Show your appreciation. Something like, "Thank you for the offer, but I have some other commitments," or "I understand your predicament; however, it's not the right time for me," or something like, "I wish to help but..."

A little appreciation and empathy, given genuinely, go a long way in making the other person feel satisfied despite having received an unfavourable response.

Offer Possible Alternatives

Where possible, offer real alternatives. Do not offer false options just to avoid the person or the discussion for the time being. For example, do not say things such as "Not right now, but maybe next week." That will only prolong the matter and leave you stressed out. On the other hand, if you have a genuine alternative in mind, such as a person who might actually be willing to take up a particular task, suggest that option.

Do Not Feel Guilty

Saying no does not make you selfish, unhelpful, or rude. You should, in fact, feel better for taking control of your time and energy, both being limited resources. You must be absolutely convinced that you are not doing wrong or being selfish by saying no. You should not feel any guilt for saying no. You would actually be doing the other person a favour. More often than not, people seek help only because they have it readily available from people such as yourself. Instead of giving something a try, they would hand it over, not because of need but for convenience.

Conclusion

In a world that often glorifies busyness, productivity, and people-pleasing, the art of saying no is a radical act of self-care and empowerment. By learning to set clear boundaries, communicate our needs, and prioritise our own well-being, we reclaim our time, energy, and autonomy, and create the space for what truly matters in our lives.

At its core, saying no is about honouring our own limits and desires, even when they conflict with the expectations or demands of others. It's about recognising that our time and attention are precious resources, and that we have the right and responsibility to allocate them in ways that align with our values, goals, and capacity. By practising discernment and self-awareness, we learn to distinguish between the opportunities that truly serve us and those that deplete or distract us from our path.

One of the key challenges of saying no is overcoming the fear of disappointing, angering, or alienating others. In a culture that often equates worth with self-sacrifice and agreeability, it can feel deeply uncomfortable to assert our own needs and preferences. But by developing the courage to communicate honestly and compassionately, we build stronger, more authentic relationships based on mutual respect and understanding. We give others the opportunity to know and support us more fully, and we model the importance of self-advocacy and self-care.

Another powerful aspect of saying no is the way it frees up space for a more intentional and fulfilling yes. When we are no longer burdened by the obligations and commitments that drain us, we have more energy, creativity, and enthusiasm to invest in the things that truly light us up. We can pursue our passions, cultivate our talents, and make a meaningful difference in the world, without the constant pressure to prove our worth through productivity and people-pleasing.

Beyond the personal benefits, the practice of saying no also has important social and cultural implications. By challenging the norms of overwork, over-commitment, and self-neglect, we contribute to a more balanced, compassionate, and sustainable way of living. We inspire others to prioritise their own well-being, and we create a ripple effect of positive change in our families, workplaces, and communities. In this way, saying no becomes an act of leadership and social responsibility, reminding us of the power we have to shape our collective values and priorities.

Ultimately, the art of saying no is a lifelong practice of self-discovery, self-trust, and self-assertion. It requires us to confront our deepest fears and insecurities and to challenge the beliefs and habits that keep us trapped in cycles of overextension and burnout. It invites us to redefine success and happiness on our own terms and to cultivate a sense of inner peace and fulfilment that is not dependent on external validation or approval.

The beauty of embracing the power of 'no' is that it creates the space for a more authentic, joyful, and purposeful 'yes'. When we learn to set clear boundaries and honour our own needs, we free ourselves to engage more fully and wholeheartedly with the people, activities, and experiences that truly nourish and inspire us. We discover that the greatest gifts we can offer the world are not our endless striving and self-sacrifice, but our unique presence, creativity, and love.

As you embark on your own journey of learning to say no, remember that it is a practice of self-love, self-respect, and self-trust. Start small, be patient with yourself, and celebrate each step forward as a victory. Surround yourself with supportive people who understand and encourage your boundaries, and trust in the wisdom of your own inner voice.

Saying no is about saying yes to a life of greater authenticity, purpose, and joy. It's about aligning our choices with our deepest values and desires and creating the space for our highest potential to unfold. By honouring our own limits and needs, we open ourselves up to a world of limitless possibility and fulfilment. And that is the greatest gift we can give ourselves and the world.

Friends

Friendship is the hardest thing in the world to explain. It's not something you learn in school. But if you haven't learned the meaning of friendship, you really haven't learned anything.

– Muhammad Ali

If life is a dish and family the ingredients, then friends are the much-needed spices. They add flavour to our lives. As we move on from school and college, the number of friends decreases, but a friendship's value increases. Over time, we are left with only a few friends, the inner circle, with whom we can share more and expect less.

We may have more than a thousand friends on social media, but we are unlikely to have more than five on our mind whom we actually consider our friends. In our 30s, the context of our friends changes, and they are no longer just fulfilling the need for fun but a more profound need for social interaction, which is vital for our inner and outer well-being.

With our thoughts and actions that follow our thoughts, we attract certain people into our lives.

Unfortunately, most are lost with time, but some stick around; those are our friends. Like most relationships, friendship is a mutual need-based relationship, but the expectations are not so high.

There is a freshness involved in this relationship. We do not live with our friends, so every time we meet some friends, there is a feeling of change, a detour from my usual course, which could otherwise become banal.

Choosing our Friends

We do not get to choose our family, but we do choose our friends. I think this is incorrect. I feel that we attract certain kinds of people into our lives. This happens through our thoughts. We end up attracting people with similar thought patterns or complementary thought patterns. For example, if you like to gossip, you will attract people who want to gossip with you. Suppose you like 'yes men' around. In that case, you will attract those 'yes men' who may be looking for their own benefits from the relationship. Therefore, with friends, it is less about choice and more about attraction.

Opposites Attract

In any kind of relationship, the concept of opposites attract is also not sustainable. Opposites may attract, but only due to the novelty attached to the differences of the two individuals. Eventually, the wonder of newness fades, and the differences persist. Therefore, some semblance is necessary for two individuals to forge a relationship. In most cases, what attracts two individuals is the similarity of the mind, the mental make-up of the two individuals.

Sort and Eliminate

Once it is established that the two share some commonality, then the rest of the things are also considered, such as social status, financial status, mannerisms, behaviour, etc. Based on your priorities or expectations, you will attract different individuals with different ratios of all the factors which you consider essential. Next, in your mind, you will run a 'sort and eliminate' programme. The same programme will be run by others who may eliminate you from their list.

The Inner Circle

Substantial permutations and combinations will take place before you reach your inner circle of friends, and that inner circle will be formed. If you are lucky, your inner circle will stick with you through thick and thin. The inner circle of friends is unlikely to be more than five. The rest will become old friends and acquaintances.

Being a Good Friend

To be a good friend, you will need to be genuinely interested in the other person's life. That bond with the other is developed with mutual respect and admiration.

Our close social circle, our inner circle, is important for developing self-worth and for our happiness. The feeling of having someone who has our back gives us a psychological boost, a sense of safety.

The trust with someone is developed over a long period. An extended period of camaraderie is needed. The connected, yet unconnected, life that we live these days prevents us from living the life of amity and trust, which requires time and effort. The average number of real friends has gone down drastically, and then, when we need someone to fall back on, we are left with nothing, which leads to dissatisfaction. The fact is that we are social animals, and we need a social circle or close allies to feel happy, safe, and satisfied with life.

Your inner circle is an integral part of your life since they are a small group of people who significantly influence you, your thoughts, and your actions. Their influence can easily surpass the power that your family may have on you.

In school, we were told that we should choose our friends wisely, yet I feel that I hardly had any choice in my set of friends at different stages of my life. It was as if they were just around me, and many of them still are, without me making any choice. So, now that I understand how it works, I will not say that you should choose your friends carefully. However, you should choose your thoughts carefully because that will define what you attract in life, including your friends.

Make sure not to take your close friends for granted. Give your relationships the time and energy they need to flourish. Every relationship is like a plant. Your encounter with another person is a seed. That seed will only grow into a plant if you put it in the soil and then water it every day, nourish it, and give it a lot of sunshine to grow into a plant. You may have many such plants, but in all likelihood, only one or two of those plants will grow into trees. These trees will have deep roots that will give them the strength to survive the rough weather, the strength to endure a few days without sunshine, and the power to not let the weeds eat into it. Identify your tree relationships among the plants and seeds, embrace them and protect them with love, care, and, more than anything, sincerity.

Conclusion

In the tapestry of human life, few threads are as vibrant, enduring, and essential as the bonds of friendship. From the playmates of our childhood to the confidants of our later years, friends are the companions who witness our triumphs, console us in our defeats, and remind us of our inherent worth and lovability. By cultivating and cherishing these precious relationships, we create a network of support, joy, and belonging that enriches every aspect of our lives.

At the heart of true friendship is a profound sense of connection, acceptance, and mutual understanding.

Friends are the people who see us as we truly are – with all our quirks, flaws, and vulnerabilities – and love us not in spite of them, but because of them. They are the ones who listen without judgement, offer wisdom without preaching, and celebrate our successes as if they were their own. In the presence of a true friend, we feel seen, heard, and valued for our authentic selves.

One of the great gifts of friendship is the way it expands our horizons and enriches our perspective. Through our friends, we encounter new ideas, experiences, and ways of being in the world. We learn to see through different lenses, to empathise with different struggles, and to find common ground across divides. In this way, friendship becomes a powerful force for personal growth, social healing, and collective transformation.

Another beautiful aspect of friendship is the way it evolves and deepens over time. As we move through the seasons of life – from the carefree days of youth to the joys and challenges of adulthood – our friendships take on new dimensions and meanings. Some friends come into our lives for a reason, a season, or a lifetime, each leaving an indelible mark on our hearts. Through the shared memories, laughter, and tears, we weave a tapestry of love and belonging that sustains us through life's ups and downs.

Beyond the personal rewards, friendship also has profound social and cultural implications. In a world that often feels fragmented and polarised, the bonds of friendship remind us of our common humanity and the power of connection to bridge divides. By extending the hand of friendship across boundaries of race, class, religion, and ideology, we create a more just, compassionate, and inclusive world. In this way, friendship becomes a revolutionary act of love and solidarity.

Ultimately, the art of friendship is a lifelong journey of giving and receiving, learning and growing, and showing up with an open heart. It requires us to cultivate the virtues of empathy, generosity, forgiveness, and vulnerability, and to invest time and energy in nurturing our relationships. It invites us to prioritise connection over transaction, and to build a life rich in love, laughter, and belonging.

The beauty of embracing the gift of friendship is that it has the power to transform not only our own lives but the world around us. When we surround ourselves with people who inspire, support, and challenge us to be our best selves, we become a force for positive change in our families, communities, and beyond. We discover that the greatest joys and triumphs in life are not those we achieve alone, but those we share with the people we love.

As you navigate the path of friendship, remember that it is a precious and sacred bond. Cherish the friends who have stood by you through thick and thin, and be open to the new connections that life brings your way. Cultivate the qualities of a true friend – loyalty, empathy, honesty, and unconditional love – and watch as your life blossoms with richness and meaning.

Friendship is a celebration of the human spirit in all its messy, beautiful complexity. It is a reminder that we are all in this together and that the greatest treasures in life are the people we hold dear. By opening our hearts to the transformative power of friendship, we create a world of greater love, compassion, and connection. And that is the most precious gift of all.

Part 3

Initiation

Where Do I Start?

Our mind is like a car windshield. External dust and dirt will fall on it every day, but they can be wiped off with little effort. If it is not done every day, then dirt and dust will get collected, and much more effort will be needed to clean it up, but it is still possible. Sometimes a stone or pebble may hit the windshield so hard that it scratches the surface or cracks it. In such a situation, if you need to get rid of the crack and see clearly, you will need to change the windshield.

Our mind is like that: external factors and influences will keep presenting themselves, which may temporarily blur our vision and thinking, but if we keep our thoughts clean, we can get over them quickly. However, if we dwell on negative thoughts and external influences for too long, it will take us more time and effort to bring our mind to its natural balanced state.

Moreover, suppose the external influence or incident has been such that it has left an indelible mark on our minds. In that case, we are unlikely to be able to see and think clearly. In that situation, we will need to change our minds by changing our thoughts, thought processes, and thought patterns.

Having read through so many aspects of life, hopefully, some of the readers would think about bringing about certain positive changes in their way of life. Having said that, many may also feel overwhelmed or conservative about bringing about so many changes. Some may even leave this book midway, thinking this is not possible. Some may try without direction and leave midway. While there will be some who may consider this to be a good read but may never even try to implement. An important question arises: where do I start?

Well, the intention of this book is to ensure, to the maximum extent possible, that each and every reader could take away something of value from this book and therefore, I am suggesting a method which could provide an excellent start to bring about change. This is applicable for any change you want to bring about in your life, whether physical or mental, external or internal. You may even bring about complete transformation. You may desire to change your habits, behaviour, outlook towards life, or anything else. Expecting long-lasting external changes without internal reworking is like expecting a car with engine problems to start working after a paint job. There cannot be a more straightforward method to bring about positive changes that you have always desired but never implemented.

Don't wait for inspiration, be the inspiration.

Don't wait for change to happen; bring the change. How do I bring about change? By changing your thoughts and your thought process. Sounds good! How does that happen? By being more conscious of your thoughts and feelings. Getting more esoteric! How does that happen?

The 8-Week Reboot Programme

Week 1

Wake up just 15 minutes earlier than your usual time. Even if you are not used to getting up any earlier and feel sleepy, just get up and sit up in your bed itself. Relax, take a few deep breaths. Keep your eyes closed and bring your awareness to your thoughts. The first thing you will observe is that you have a lot of thoughts running in your head. Start observing your thoughts. Don't do anything about them; just witness. It doesn't matter what kind of thoughts you're having, good, bad, or ugly; inspiring, depressing, or outright dirty. Just sit back and observe as if you are watching a movie. Once you've done that for 15 minutes, get up and start your day with the intention to be happy and calm. Do this for a week.

Week 2

Add 15 minutes of observing your thoughts before you go to sleep.

A few times during the day, while you are going about your usual routine, bring your awareness to your breath and acknowledge the life force within you. If needed, add a few reminders on your phone for this.

Then, at night, as you close your eyes, be grateful for the day gone by.

Week 3

In week 3, you will start your meditation practice. Instead of sitting and observing your thoughts for 15 minutes before bedtime, close your eyes and bring your awareness to your breath. Thoughts will keep coming, in the same manner you have been observing them for the past two weeks. The critical aspect is to keep bringing your attention back to the breath. Initially, it may seem impossible, but you need to keep at it.

Week 4

Start a 15-minute meditation routine in the morning as well.

Week 5

Add affirmations to your morning and evening routines. Divide your time to spend three parts on meditation and one part on affirmations. For example, if you have 20 minutes, spend 15 minutes on meditation and 5 minutes on affirmations.

For your affirmations, make a list of all the positive changes you wish to bring about in yourself and your life. For example, suppose your list looks like this:

I do not want to be fearful of change.
I want to be successful.

I want to be confident.
I want to be more joyful and happy.
I do not want to be affected by how others treat me.
I want to be peaceful.
I do not want to be affected by others' opinions of me.
I want to be fit and healthy.
I want to be less irritated by others.

Affirmations are always in the present tense and are prepared in a manner such that whatever you are affirming already exists in you and in your life. From the above list, you can prepare your affirmations by converting these expected changes into something which already exists, such as:

I am courageous, and I embrace change.
I am successful. I am an achiever. All my desires are fulfilled.
I am confident. I am respected. I am an inspiration for others.
I am always joyful and happy. Happiness follows me wherever I go.
I am at peace with myself. Calmness is my natural state.
I am in control of myself, my thoughts, and my feelings. I make good decisions.
People respect me. My opinion matters. I matter.
I am healthy. My body is my temple, and I take care of it. I have a healthy lifestyle. I exercise regularly, and I only eat nutritious food.

Once you have prepared your list of affirmations, you can either memorise them or record them on your phone and listen to them anytime, especially after your morning and evening meditation routines.

Week 6

While you are working on bringing about inner change, start taking small steps to bring about external changes as well:

- Avoid eating anything after 7 p.m.
- Call your spouse to tell them that you love them
- Spend extra time with your kids
- Delegate non-essential tasks at work
- Cut downtime spent on social media
- Dispose of old electronic devices

Week 7

By week 7, you would have become more conscious of your thoughts and feelings, at least during your morning and evening routines. Now, you will need to take steps to be aware of your thoughts and feelings throughout the day.

Spend a few brief moments to pay attention to how you are feeling and to your thoughts at your breakfast table, on your way to work, at work, in your meetings, at lunch, on your way back from the office, and at the dinner table.

Take some more small steps, small changes in habits and behaviour which help you reach towards your health, personal, and professional goals, such as:

- Add 30 minutes of regular moderate exercising
- Find a chore you and your partner could work on together
- Cut downtime spent on TV content
- Pick up a book you have been meaning to read for the longest time and start reading, even if it is for 15-20 minutes a day

Week 8

This week, as you make yourself aware of your thoughts and feelings at different points of the day, you need to manoeuvre your thoughts and feelings in line with your affirmations. Guide your thoughts towards positivity, success, and prosperity. Listen to positive, inspiring words on your way to work and back. Redirect any negative conversations at work or home towards something neutral or positive.

As you learn to reframe and manoeuvre your thoughts, start to experience bliss, positive energy, and happiness in your life.

Most of us live our lives or are taught to live our lives without giving any thought to our thoughts. The same is the case with our feelings. If we are having negative thoughts, we feel negative emotions like sadness, anger, or even helplessness. If we are having positive thoughts, we feel positive emotions such as happiness or excitement. The problem is that our thoughts and feelings are linked entirely to our external environment. Something good happens to us, we get positive thoughts and emotions, we feel lucky and blessed. Something terrible happens, and we think and feel the opposite.

The Reboot Programme helps you get out of that cycle. It helps you from being a slave to your thoughts and emotions to become their master. When you are more conscious of your thoughts, you gain the ability to manoeuvre them. You can guide them towards finding peace in adversity and finding positivity in a hostile environment, which should be the ultimate goal. Everything else will follow. You would have moulded your thoughts and, therefore, your life for happiness. Everyday instances will not annoy you. You will be at peace with your surroundings and your life and start attracting positive experiences in your life.

We all get two lives. One that we are born into and the second that we make for ourselves. Unfortunately, most of us end up living just one life, and then a few are brave enough to dream and brave enough to build a new life for themselves. Your second life starts only when you let go of your previous life, when you dare to get out of the past, when you start living in the present and building a new future for yourself.

Many are unable to discover their second shot at life. Many find it very late in life. However, in our 30s, we are at the perfect time to rediscover ourselves and reboot our life. It is the time when we would want to format our hard disk and rewrite the code. The ideal time to do that is in our 30s when we are well-placed to use a second life after discovering ourselves.

Our past life was a result of our environment and past choices. For most of us, most of our past decisions were made unconsciously. Today, we can choose to go along with whatever life brings to us or choose to be creators of our lives. We can choose to be self-aware and take control of our thoughts and, therefore, of our life.

Conclusion

In the face of life's countless possibilities and challenges, it's easy to feel overwhelmed and paralysed by the question of where to begin. Whether we're embarking on a new project, pursuing a long-held dream, or simply trying to navigate the complexities of daily life, the starting point can often feel elusive and daunting. But by breaking down our goals into manageable steps, cultivating a mindset of curiosity and experimentation, and trusting in the power of small beginnings, we can find the clarity, courage, and momentum to take that first leap.

At the heart of any meaningful journey is a sense of purpose and intention. Before we can begin, we must first get clear on what truly matters to us – our values, passions, and aspirations. By taking the time to reflect on our deepest desires and motivations, we create a roadmap for our lives that is authentic, inspiring, and worth pursuing. This clarity of purpose becomes our north star, guiding us through the inevitable twists and turns of the journey ahead.

Another key to starting well is embracing a spirit of experimentation and iteration. Rather than waiting for the perfect plan or the ideal circumstances, we can begin where we are, with what we have, and trust in the power of small, consistent actions to build momentum over time. By approaching our goals with a sense of curiosity and openness, we create space for learning, growth, and unexpected discoveries along the way.

One of the most powerful tools for getting started is the art of breaking down our goals into manageable, bite-sized steps. By chunking our aspirations into smaller, more achievable milestones, we make the journey feel less daunting and more accessible. We can celebrate each small victory along the way, building confidence and motivation as we go. And by focusing on the next right step, rather than the enormity of the end goal, we cultivate a sense of presence and progress that sustains us through the ups and downs.

Beyond the practical strategies, starting well also requires a certain mindset and disposition. It means cultivating the courage to face our fears and doubts, and to take risks in the pursuit of what matters most. It means surrounding ourselves with supportive people who believe in our potential and challenge us to grow. And it means practising self-compassion and patience, remembering that every journey begins with a single step, and that setbacks and detours are a natural part of the process.

Ultimately, the art of beginning is a lifelong practice of aligning our actions with our deepest values and truths. It is a commitment to showing up for ourselves and our dreams, even when the path is unclear or the obstacles seem insurmountable. It is a reminder that we are all works in progress, and that the journey itself is the destination.

The beauty of embracing the power of beginning is that it opens up a world of possibility and potential. When we take that first step, no matter how small or tentative, we set in motion a chain reaction of growth, discovery, and transformation. We learn to trust in the unfolding of our lives and to find joy and meaning in the process, not just the outcome.

As you contemplate your own starting point, remember that the most important thing is to begin. Trust in the wisdom of your own heart and in the power of small, consistent actions to create big changes over time. Surround yourself with people and practices that inspire and support you, and be willing to experiment, iterate, and adapt as you go.

The journey of a thousand miles begins with a single step. By embracing the art of beginning, we open ourselves up to a life of greater purpose, passion, and possibility. And that is the most exciting adventure of all.

May your choice take you on the path of a seeker rather than a follower.

Your Story

This book is about you. Let the end of this book be a new beginning for you. Start your journey here by penning down your thoughts. Write about thoughts and feelings, about what inspires you, about the people in your life and on your mind. Write about things you want to change in your life and things you wish to change in yourself. Write about the habits you want to release and practices you want to replace them with.

With this exercise, not only will you gain insights about yourself, but you will also experience the therapeutic effects of journaling. There has never been and can never be a better time to bring about positive change in yourself than right now. Yesterday is already over, and tomorrow is speculation, but you are here now. Your reboot begins here and now.

Notes

➢ Notes ◄

About the Author

Abhinav Bhalla is a lawyer, writer, and seeker of meaning in the madness of modern life. Born and raised in Faridabad, India, he embarked on a transformative journey of self-discovery and growth in his thirties.

With a background in law and a passion for understanding the human experience, Abhinav has spent the last decade navigating the challenges and joys of adulthood, parenthood, and the pursuit of purpose. He is a keen observer of life and has a talent for distilling complex insights into relatable and empowering wisdom.

In his legal practice, Abhinav has worked with a diverse range of clients, gaining a deep understanding of the struggles and triumphs that define the human condition. He brings this wealth of experience and empathy to his writing, offering a fresh and authentic perspective on the universal challenges of modern life.

When he's not writing or practising law, you can find Abhinav exploring new places, learning new skills, or spending time with his children who continue to be his greatest teachers and sources of inspiration.

'The Thirties' Reboot' is Abhinav's first book, born from a desire to share the hard-won lessons and insights of his own journey and to inspire others to embrace the transformative power of this pivotal decade. He hopes this book will be a companion and guide for anyone seeking to live a more authentic, purposeful and joyful life.